JANELLE WEST

You Thought...

CORRECTING WHAT WE THINK WE KNOW ABOUT GOD AND CHRISTIANITY

You Thought...

CORRECTING WHAT WE THINK WE KNOW ABOUT GOD AND CHRISTIANITY

JANELLE WEST

You Thought

Correcting What We Think We Know About God and Christianity
© 2019, Janelle West
Anointed Fire™ House
(info@anointedfire.com)

ALL RIGHTS RESERVED. This book contains material protected under International and Federal Copyright Laws and Treaties. Any unauthorized reprint or use of this material is prohibited. No part of this book may be reproduced or transmitted in any form or by any means, electronic or mechanical, including photocopying, recording, or by any information storage and retrieval system without express written permission from the author / publisher.

Disclaimer

This book is designed to provide information and motivation to our readers. It is sold with the understanding that the publisher is not engaged to render any type of psychological, legal, or any other kind of professional advice. No warranties or guarantees are expressed or implied by the author, since every man has his own measure of faith. The individual author(s) shall not be liable for any physical, psychological, emotional, financial, or commercial damages, including; but not limited to, special, incidental, consequential or other damages. Our views and rights are the same: You are responsible for your own choices, actions, and results.

ISBN: 978-1-7331127-3-4

Dedicated to "My little stink" and.....to all people who accepted me when no one else did, showed me love when I felt neglected, and have been there for me in my darkest hours. This is my gift to you. I thank God every day that I have had the pleasure of having you guys in my life. I pray that this book finds you in some way and that it blesses you! You know who you are 😊. I love you so much.

TABLE OF CONTENTS

INTRODUCTION..IX

   THE HOLY TRINITY...1

   GOD, THE FATHER 7

   GOD, THE SON: JESUS CHRIST..............................21

   GOD, THE HOLY SPIRIT 43

   THE BIBLE...57

   PRAYER...73

   FAITH..83

   PRAISE AND WORSHIP...95

   SATAN, OUR ENEMY...145

   LISTS 193

INTRODUCTION

Oh my gosh! I cannot believe you're reading my first book! I'm so glad that you decided to pick it up! Thank you and I love you! The reason I wrote this book for you (yes, you) was because, after committing my life to Jesus Christ, it dawned on me that a lot of people either don't understand the basics of Christianity or have the wrong idea about who God and Jesus are. I mean, He was revealing one wrong ideology after another that not just I had, but most people I knew had as well. I really felt in my heart that God was leading me to share this with you. I wanted to correct the Christian myths and assumptions that are out there. The last thing I want is for someone to turn away from Jesus Christ simply because they don't know the truth about who He is. So, I'm here to clear some of that up for you! I'm no big-time scholar with a million degrees in literature. I'm not here to be judgmental, critical, or use big fancy words. I'm just regular girl from Jersey (REPRESENT) here to share the truth with you in a clear way so everyone will be able to understand. Good? Let's get started then!

Really quick, I want to go over how I've laid this book out. I've divided it into three sections, the first section is on THE TRINITY and certain aspects of Christianity, such as faith and salvation. The second section focuses on the changes that come with being a Christian, and the third section is on the enemy, Satan. Before each topic is discussed, I placed questions for you to answer to see what you know about Christianity now. At the end of each section, there will be another set of questions to fill out so you can gauge what you've learned from what you've read. I hope this helps you out and you're able to seek a deeper relationship and meaning of who God and Jesus Christ are.

The first question is, what do you know about Christianity now? Really think on this and be honest with yourself. Go over any and everything you know about it (literally), including bad experiences with church, Christian family members, and every experience you've had. Jot some ideas down, and then, we'll go into who God is.

WHAT I KNOW NOW
What do you know about Christianity now?
What are your thoughts and feelings when it first comes to mind?

_____

_____

_____

_____

_____

_____

_____

THE HOLY TRINITY

One of the first things that God showed me was the significant differences between knowing Him and knowing of Him. A lot of us know OF Him, but can we really say that we KNOW Him? What's the difference?

KNOWING OF HIM
- Know the facts about Him.
    - From friends, family.
- No relationship with Him/don't know Him intimately.
    - No communication.

KNOWING HIM
- Have a close, intimate relationship with Him.
    - Experiencing Him for yourself.
- Put Him first in all decisions.

You cannot truly know who He is just by hearing about other people's testimonies, and you cannot know Him just because your family knows Him. My family and church friends would try to explain to me who Jesus is, but it never really sunk in until I had my first one-on-one encounter with Him. It's hard for you to pray to and ask someone for something who you don't know. Until you see God at work in your life and have your eyes opened to how He has been with you all of this time and until you see and hear Him in your life on a daily basis, you won't really know who He is. It helps you to come to grips with how deeply He loves you. You have to feel and be in His presence and get that overwhelming sense of peace after you have prayed to Him. Embrace the hope that He gives you when you're worried about something. God will also reveal Himself to every believer differently. He may speak to you through a Scripture or through another fellow believer who is witnessing to you. With me, it was feeling His presence and hearing His voice deep down in my spirit that made me realize how real He is. You receive it through faith.

Now, what do you know about God already? What were you told or what have you heard about Him?

WHAT I KNOW NOW
Who is God? What do you know about Him?

To start off, God is composed of three different persons, also known as the Godhead or the Holy Trinity. Yeah, I know what you're thinking … "How the heck is that possible? It doesn't even make sense!" I know, because I've been there. There is really no clear way to explain it, but I've heard of two illustrations that make it a bit easier for me to understand. Instead of looking at the Trinity as addition (1+1+1=3), it is better to view it as multiplication (1x1x1=1). The other example I saw was looking at the Holy Trinity like a three-leaf clover. You have one stem that has three separate leaves. It is one God manifesting Himself into three persons. They are God (the Father), God, (the Son: Jesus Christ), and God (the Holy Spirit).

SCRIPTURE REFERENCES TO THE HOLY TRINITY

In the Old Testament, Genesis 1:26 says, "Then God said,

The Holy Trinity

"Let us make mankind in our image, in our likeness..." In the New Testament, Jesus (God, The Son) mentions both God, the Father and the Holy Spirit (Luke 3:22, John 5:26).

- 1st Corinthians 8:6: yet for us there is but one God, the Father, from whom all things came and for whom we live; and there is but one Lord, Jesus Christ, through whom all things came and through whom we live.
- 2nd Corinthians 13:14: May the grace of the **Lord Jesus Christ, and the love of God, and the fellowship of the Holy Spirit be with you all.**
- Genesis 1:1-2: In the beginning, God created the heaven and the earth. And the earth was without form, and void; and darkness was upon the face of the deep. And the **Spirit** of God moved upon the face of the waters.
- Matthew 28:9: Go therefore and make disciples of all the nations, baptizing them in the name of **the Father and the Son and the Holy Spirit."**

Each "person" of the Godhead has a different function, but they are all equal in essence. One didn't exist before the other and one doesn't have more power than the other. They are all connected. Here are a few characteristics that the Holy Trinity share:

- perfect/sinless/holy (Mark 10:18)
- no physical body
    >spirit/ invisible (John 1:18, Colossians 1:15)
- all-loving (Psalms 136:26, Psalms 86:5)
- eternal, was never created/always existed (Isaiah 40:28, Deuteronomy 33:27, Isaiah 44:6)
    >Whatever He decides to do is imprinted in history

for all of eternity (Deuteronomy 33:27, Job 36:26)
- all-knowing/omniscient (Isaiah 46:9-10, Psalms 147: 4-5)
- always present/omnipresent (Proverbs 15:3)
- all-powerful/omnipotent (Isaiah 44:24, Psalms 147:5)
- relational being (doesn't need a relationship with us, He WANTS it)

I remember it frustrated me so much that I couldn't fully understand how the Trinity was possible. I was really hard on myself because I didn't understand how God could have three Persons, but still be one God. God revealed something to me that we all have to realize, and I know you may not want to hear this, but we aren't supposed to understand the Holy Trinity to the fullest because it is an eternal concept and our minds are not equipped to understand eternity or spiritual things. I heard somewhere that God is not meant to be deconstructed. There is no possible way for us to completely grasp the whole concept of His existence and power. We can spend all our lives trying to figure Him out and we wouldn't even scratch the surface of His infinite power and knowledge. This truth is difficult for the human mind to accept, because we can't totally understand the Trinity, nevertheless, God's Word teaches us to just believe that it so. Yeah, I know what some of you are thinking. How can we just accept and believe something when we don't have all the facts? At some point, we're gonna have to realize that we can ask a million questions about God and Christianity as a whole (and I definitely encourage you to do so), but we simply need to have faith and accept that the answers are not always in black and white. We're human!! We don't know everything, nor do we have the answers to everything! Again, it goes back to us being temporal and God being eternal. There are some things about His nature that God will reveal to us, and there are other things that He won't reveal. There are some things we just have to take by faith without fully understanding them (look out for another book from me answering a lot of common, controversial questions we all have about Christianity). Give yourself some time to recap and see what you just learned about the Holy Trinity.

WHAT I'VE LEARNED
What have I just learned about the Holy Trinity that I didn't know before?

Intro to The Holy Trinity...CHECK! Let's move on to God, the Father; shall we?

GOD, THE FATHER

An old white guy sporting a big old white beard, wearing a white robe and standing in the clouds. I don't know about you, but this is what comes to mind when I think of God, the Father. Yep, that's about right. I always thought that He was controlling, unsympathetic, unkind, and unforgiving. Just "un" everything. I don't think I'm alone in this either… Who do YOU think He is?

WHAT I KNOW NOW
Who is God, the Father?

God, the Father

Who He is

Most importantly, He is the "first person" of the Trinity. Everything flows and originates through Him. This is why we witness Jesus (God, the Son) saying in the Word that He was SENT by His Father. John 14:31 says, "But he comes so that the world may learn that I love the Father and do exactly what my Father has commanded me." The world likes to paint this picture of Him like He's not approachable or relatable—like He's too busy to care about our small, insignificant lives with everything else He has to do. I mean, He is making sure that everything in the universe keeps spinning and working right, which is kind of a big job, you know? Let's go through some of the things that describe Him in the Bible. Oh, and before we get into what He is like, I found that by thinking of Him literally as your eternal Father, all of His qualities will make perfect sense and they'll kind of fit together better. Let's get into it...

What is He like/His nature
- ✓ **He is patient.** (Numbers 14:18: "The Lord is slow to anger, abounding in love and forgiving sin and rebellion.") This is so important on a number of levels. For one, God doesn't want anyone to be eternally lost and separated from Him, so His patience allows us time to receive His gift of salvation (which I will get into within the next few chapters) and have an intimate relationship with Him. Next, it allows time for repentance (meaning to turn away from your sins, ask for forgiveness, and obey God). And lastly, His patience gives us time to correct our mistakes and learn from them. I can tell you right now, there have

been so many times where God has tried to tell me something and I either didn't want to listen or I didn't understand what He was saying. Even after it took me a long time to see it, He waited patiently for me to understand and do what He was telling me to do. I thank Him that He's not like us, because I know I would've given up on me a long time ago. This is who God REALLY is, and I'm only scratching the surface. We'll delve deeper into this subject as we go along.

2 Peter 3:9: The Lord is not slow in keeping his promise, as some understand slowness. Instead, he is patient with you, not wanting anyone to perish, but everyone to come to repentance.

- ✓ **He is loyal and faithful.** (1 John 5:14-15: And this is the confidence that we have in him, that, if we ask anything according to his will, he heareth us: And if we know that he hear us, whatsoever we ask, we know that we have the petitions that we desired of him.) Let's first reexamine what it actually means to be faithful, because Lord knows with the way people are acting nowadays, we need a little refresher. The word "faithful" means that someone will be true to their word. They are reliable and trusted. This is our Father! He never breaks a promise and He is always here for us! Even when other people leave and abandon us, our Father will always be there! He will answer every prayer and provide for every single one of our needs. Here's a list of some of the promises God speaks of in His Word:

God, the Father

> **Isaiah 40:29:** He gives strength to the weary and increases the power of the weak.
> **Isaiah 41:10:** So, do not fear, for I am with you; do not be dismayed, for I am your God. I will strengthen you and help you; I will uphold you with my righteous right hand.
> **James 1:5:** If any of you lacks wisdom, you should ask God, who gives generously to all without finding fault, and it will be given to you.
> **2 Thessalonians 3:3:** But the Lord is faithful. He will establish you and guard you against the evil one
> **Deuteronomy 7:9:** Know therefore that the Lord thy God, He is God, the faithful God, which keepeth covenant and mercy with them that love Him and keep His commandments to a thousand generations.)

Look around you for a minute. If you have all of your needs met (shelter, food, clothes), God is still faithful to you! And if you ever need reassurance of His faithfulness, look throughout the Old Testament of the Bible. Oh my gosh, this is so major. Since the fall of Adam and Eve, He promised to send the world a Savior who would deliver them from sin and grant them eternal life, right? He fulfilled that promise when He sent His Son to die for us on the cross. He could've gone back on His Word, but He didn't. He CHOSE to send His Son as a sacrifice for you and me.

- ✓ **He is our Provider.** (Philippians 4:19: And my God will supply every need of yours according to His riches in glory in Christ Jesus.) Because God is loyal and faithful, you can trust that He will keep His promise in providing for your needs! From simple everyday needs to an opportunity you need to advance through life, God will always find a way to provide it for you. Give yourself a minute and look around you. Are you still breathing? Do you have clothes on your back? Did you even have the money to buy this book? Yep, He's still providing for you! Look at me, for example. While I was writing this book, He PROVIDED me with a roof over my head, a car to drive, food, and the opportunity to save money, all the while working on a part time job. He PROVIDED the right living conditions for me to write this book for you! He has gone above and beyond for me. I didn't need to worry because He got me covered every single time! You don't need to worry either!

Psalms 37:25: Yet have I not seen the righteous forsaken, nor his seed begging for bread.

Matthew 6:31-34: So do not worry, saying, 'What shall we eat?' or 'What shall we drink?' or 'What shall we wear?' For the pagans run after all these things, and your heavenly Father knows that you need them. But seek first his kingdom and his righteousness, and all these things will be given to you as well. Therefore do not worry about tomorrow, for tomorrow will worry about itself. Each day has enough trouble of its own.

- ✓ **God, the Father, is caring.** Before I really knew who He was, when I was dealing with something that had me feeling frustrated or upset, I just pictured Him sitting in Heaven shrugging His shoulders and pretty much saying,

God, the Father

"Get over it." It's funny how I used to believe that God never cared about my feelings or desires. Oh my gosh, was I wrong! He cares about us so much, it is insane! He is the complete and total opposite. He doesn't like to see you mad or upset. Look at what He calls us—we're His *children*. He doesn't call us His slaves, He doesn't call us anything that's deemed as unworthy of love and care. Instead, He calls us His children.

Psalm 34:17-20: When the righteous cry for help, the Lord hears and delivers them out of all their troubles. The Lord is near to the brokenhearted and saves the crushed in spirit. Many are the afflictions of the righteous, but the Lord delivers him out of them all. He keeps all his bones; not one of them is broken.

- ✓ **He's our Comforter.** From the smallest irritations that bug you throughout the day to the things that you have been struggling with for years, He cares about it all. When you begin to see God taking care of really small things in your life, you'll begin to realize just how much He cares, and it helps you to build a closer relationship with Him. He cares about it all. Watch Him start taking care of those small, itty-bitty things in your life and you'll begin to understand just how much He cares.

Testimony: I remember one week at my job when I had been scheduled to work in a department that I could not stand working in. I said a small prayer that God would just give me the strength to get through the week in one piece and not self-destruct (I work in retail). I just kept telling myself in the days leading up to my shift that God wouldn't allow the week to be too bad. It turned out that the day after that prayer, my manager asked if I wouldn't mind switching departments. I was elated. You don't know how intensely I was praising His name and thanking Him. He'd answered my prayer! He was listening! He'd heard something that, to most, would be so small and insignificant. I just never thought He would actually do it. I have many more stories of Him just showing me little acts of kindness. I could fill a whole other book up with them! It just shows me how awesome of a job He does at taking care of His kids. Just read this one passage of scripture. Luke 12:7: Indeed, the very hairs of your head are all numbered.

Don't be afraid; you are worth more than many sparrows. If He knows how many hairs are on your head, trust and believe that He cares about the smallest things that happen to you throughout your day. We can trust Him. Let your Father comfort you!

> **2nd Corinthians 1: 3-5:** Blessed be the God and Father of our Lord Jesus Christ, the Father of mercies and God of all comfort, who comforts us in all our affliction, so that we may be able to comfort those who are in any affliction, with the comfort with which we ourselves are comforted by God.

- ✓ There was no way I could leave out this next point because it is so relevant to what we're experiencing in society right now, and we all need to be reminded of this. **Our Father is not racist, sexist, or classist. He shows no favoritism and**

does not look at the outward appearance. He looks inward at your heart. 1 Samuel 16:7 reads, "But the Lord said to Samuel, 'Do not look on his appearance or on the height of his stature, because I have rejected him. For the Lord sees not as man sees man looks on the outward appearance, but the Lord looks on the heart.'" Whoever accepts His Son as their Savior will be able to form a relationship with our Father. ALL humans were made in the image of God. Genesis 1:26 says, "And God said, Let us make man in our image, after our likeness." If He made us all in His image, why would He only save or bless certain people? There are tons of stories in His Word of Him using different classes, races and genders of people to carry out His will. He used a widow and a prostitute! Paul killed Christians and He wrote most of the New Testament! There're even several accounts in the Bible that speak on Jesus ministering to women and people of different nationalities (See John 4:4-26, Luke 10:25-37). Our Father does not discriminate. He loves and wants to save all of us.

    Romans 2:11: God shows no partiality.

- ✓ **Our Father is just, yet merciful.** He will always fight for you and He will not and cannot let sin go unpunished. Our Father is all-knowing and sees all that we go through, right? So, when He sees you being abused, mistreated, or anything like that, He will not turn a blind eye to it. He hates to see His kids hurting, just like any other father would. So, don't worry about getting revenge; it is not your responsibility! Don't go seeking your own revenge, love. God's got it covered. Romans 12:19 reads, "Do not take revenge, my dear friends, but leave room for God's wrath, for it is written: 'It is mine to avenge; I will repay,' says the Lord." Like I said before, God cannot let sin go unpunished. Which includes EVERYONE. Yes, this goes for you too. Romans 3:23 reads, "For all have sinned, and come short of the glory of God." And because of His mercy, when we accept Christ as our Savior, He doesn't give us what we deserve. The definition of mercy is, "compassion or forgiveness shown toward someone whom it is within one's power to punish or harm." We would all be separated from Him for eternity if He didn't send His Son to die for us.

> **1 Corinthians 15:58:** Therefore, my beloved brethren, be ye steadfast, unmovable, always abounding in the work of the Lord, forasmuch as ye know that your labor is not in vain in the Lord.
>
> **2 Thessalonians 1:6:** God is just: He will pay back trouble to those who trouble you.
>
> **Deuteronomy 32:4:** He is the Rock, his works are perfect, and all his ways are just. A faithful God who does no wrong, upright and just is He.

- ✓ **He is our Protector.** Think for a second of God literally acting as your father. What do good fathers do for their kids? Protect them! He wants to shield them from all kinds of evil. What do you think God does for us? Sometimes, it may not look like He's protecting us, though. He can be shielding us from something, even when that something looks like an open door or a good opportunity. Look at it this way. For example, natural fathers see much more than their children see because they are more mature. Isn't that like us? He has an infinite amount of knowledge that we, His children, do not possess. So, when He takes something away from us, it looks like we are being punished. Because of this, we start getting mad and pouting like children do. There have been so many times when I thought that an opportunity seemed really convenient or right for me, be it career-wise or relationship-wise, but God removed it from my life. I would sit there feeling confused. I'd think to myself, "Why was this perfect chance taken away from me? It would have solved so many of my problems!" But what we have to do is trust in Him when He says "no" to things or takes something away from us. It's all out of love, just like a dad would do for his children here on Earth. Just imagine how many things He has protected you from! Psalms 91 is an amazing passage in the Old Testament that gives a detailed explanation of how God wants to be your protector.

Testimony: One morning, I woke up and started checking my social media pages. Every status and meme I saw was about the recent, racially driven police shootings that had been occurring. I started crying uncontrollably from fear and anxiety as I looked at my son sleeping next to me. I really feared for his life and began to worry that I wouldn't be able to protect him from all the evil in this world. I immediately cried out to God, asking Him to give me peace of mind and to protect my family and myself. Almost incautiously, something in my spirit told me to calm down and not to worry. Shielding my son from hurt, harm, or danger is HIS job. Shortly afterward, my dad and I had a brief conversation about what was going on in our country. He pretty much repeated what that small voice had told me beforehand. I believe that God spoke through my dad that morning to reassure me that He has everything in control.

- ✓ **He is our ultimate Healer.** There's a ton of stories in the Word of God where people have been physically healed, and I've seen and heard about people getting healed from sicknesses and diseases. But He's not just a physical healer. If you open your heart to Him and still yourself to listen to His direction, God will give you physical, mental and emotional healing. He's able to heal the things and issues we cannot see as well! He's the supernatural Healer! God is our Healer, and His Word is our medicine. His Word is a cure for every sickness and disease (I'll go into the different ways God heals us later in this book). He wants to rid you of every past hurt you've experienced and replace it with His love, dear one! He wants to grow and mature you!

    Psalms 103:2-3: Bless the LORD, O my soul, and forget not all His benefits: Who forgives all your iniquities, Who heals all your diseases.

- ✓ One of the most amazing things that I've come to love about our Father is that **He wants an intimate relationship with us.** Just think, the Creator of the universe wants you to speak with Him, and He wants to get close to you! We really need to be upset with Adam and Eve for messing up our chances of still having the close relationship they had with God. The Father's name means exactly that. He wants an intimate parent/child relationship with you. He wants to provide us with the guidance and protection that a father would to His children. He will provide you with the answers to your problems and tell you what you should or shouldn't do, just like you would want your father to. He also wants to be the first person you come to with your problems. He desires for you to trust Him enough that you bring all your frustrations to Him and be completely open and honest. Imagine that.

- ✓ **He is all-loving.** In reality, God IS love!! He loves everything and everyone in the whole universe. I've heard somewhere that God's love is uncaused. For example, look at us. We often love based on attraction, right? Well, God loves you regardless. His love isn't based on anything. With Him, there is no "I love you because..." He just does! He loves you when you're at your absolute worst and when you're at your best. He loves every Atheist, Muslim, and Buddhist. Just think about that for a second. Even if you deny His existence or choose to follow another religion, He still loves you. 1 Corinthians 13:4-7 is my favorite scripture; it lists all of the things that love is. It is right here (I believe) that you also get a clear explanation of who the Father is. Since God is love, this scripture literally lists all of the things that He is! I can give you countless scriptures that support this trait of God the Father, but here are a few.

1 John 4:8: Anyone who does not love does not know God, because God is love.

1 John 4:16: So, we have come to know and to believe the love that God has for us. God is love, and whoever abides in love abides in God, and God abides in him.

1 John 4:7: Beloved, let us love one another, for love is from God, and whoever loves has been born of God and knows God.

He is the best Father you could ask for. For anyone who is reading this that grew up without a father, please know that our eternal Father is the only one you need! He loved us so much that He sent His only Son to die in our place! He demonstrated the ultimate act of love for all mankind—past, present, and future. We don't have to be separated from God now because of Jesus Christ. Which leads us into the next person of the Holy Trinity. We are moving right along ya'll, so stay with me. But before you read ahead, write down what you've learned about God, the Father, real quick.

WHAT HAVE I LEARNED ABOUT GOD, THE FATHER?

God, the Father

GOD, THE SON: JESUS CHRIST

Okay, you know the drill by now. Give yourself some time to write out what you already know about Jesus. Have you heard about Him through family members, or do you only know Him because of Christmas songs? Be honest and write everything that comes to mind.

<u>WHAT I KNOW NOW</u>
Who is Jesus Christ? What do you know about Him already?

God, the Son: Jesus Christ

Here's a list of the general facts about Him:
- He lived for 33 years.
- John 3:16.
- He was born of the virgin Mary in a manager.
- He was born in Bethlehem and grew up in Nazareth.
- He was a carpenter.
- He died on the cross and rose again on the third day.
- And here's an extra bonus fact: He is John, the Baptist's cousin! (Yeah, I didn't know that one either).

For me personally, I grew up knowing that Jesus Christ died for our sins, was buried and rose again on the third day, and that pretty much summed it up. I never really grasped the reason "why" He died for us, so I just settled on the idea that He was nothing more than a prophet or a good teacher like Mohammed from Islam. I didn't see the significance in believing that He is the Son of God and how that would grant me eternal life. Even in the beginning stages of my salvation, I had so many questions about who He was and why He died. I didn't understand why it was a MUST that, in order to get into Heaven, I needed to really believe in my heart that He exists and has saved me. I always asked myself, "Saved me from what? What have I done that He needs to save me from?" This goes back to knowing Him versus knowing of Him.
Let's get more familiar with exactly who He is first.

A DEEPER LOOK INTO WHO HE IS
- ✓ **Jesus Christ is the living Word of God, the Father.** He's been there right alongside God, the Father, ever since the

beginning. The opening to the book of John reveals to the reader that Jesus is eternal like the rest of the Holy Trinity (John 1:1-14). He existed first as the Word of God, then God made His Word into flesh (or Jesus Christ). This ties back into how He is 100% God. When God created the universe, He spoke words and everything came into existence (Genesis 1:1-5). And John tells us that Jesus is the living Word of God. So, through Christ, all of life was made! It's crazy, right? God chose His Son to be the means by which life itself would be created.

- ✓ **He is 100% God and 100% human.** His human name is Jesus, but Christ is His deity (Christ means "anointed/chosen one"). Jesus being one hundred percent God is a reminder that He is a Person in the Godhead—He always was and always will be. He had to be human in order to pay the price for all of us. By Him being human, it also gives Him another way to relate to us. We always think of Christ as part of the Trinity (His deity), but don't remember that He was also human just like us. He got hungry like us (Luke 24:41-43), cried like us (John 11:35), and needed to sleep like us (Mark 4:38). He couldn't die unless He became a man, His Son, Jesus Christ. To this day, He still retains both natures (Luke 24:39, 24:50-51)! He is the flesh of the eternal living God.

- ✓ **Jesus is also known as the "Bread of Life" (John 6:35), the "Light of the World" (John 8:12), and the "Water of Life" (John 6:35).** I remember seeing a meme on Facebook talking about this. It said that we need food, light, and water to survive. Guess who contains all of these things? What this means is when you drink and eat Him (or when you let Him into your life), you will never go hungry or thirst again, meaning, He will provide all of your needs. When you put Him first or consume Him on a daily basis through prayer and reading the Bible, your every need will be met. You become satisfied (full) just by having Him in your life. Let me break it down a little more. Everyone knows water is an extremely vital source of life for our bodies. When God, the Son, is referred to as the "Water of Life," it means that He is an essential part of your life. You need water every day to survive and you need Christ every day to survive. Bread is considered a signature food item for every meal in any county in the world, and is a major food in Jewish culture. Christ used this symbolism when telling people who He was to stress to them how important He is. When it comes to Him being the Light of the world, it means that He shows us where to go in life. Following and listening to His truth guides and leads us as we live in this world. When we walk in this world that is filled with darkness, He acts as the light to our paths to lead us down the right way. Here's the meme by the way (see next page):

God, the Son: Jesus Christ

> **Science says that we need at least 4 basic elements to survive.**
>
> 1. Water
> 2. Air
> 3. Food
> 4. Light
>
> **And look what the Bible tells us about Jesus:**
>
> 1. I am the sourde of living water.
> 2. I am the breath of life.
> 3. I am the bread of life.
> 4. I am the light of the world.
>
> **Science was right, we need JESUS to LIVE!**
> Lury

(Source: https://me.me/i/science-says-that-4-basic-eleme-we-rieed-at-leasi-20970874)

✓ **WHY DID HE NEED TO DIE ON THE CROSS?**

In order to answer this, we have to go back in time and look at how it all started.

- **THE FALL/THE FIRST SIN**

I think we're all familiar with the story of Adam and Eve, right? If not, here's the rundown of it (you can read about it more in Genesis 2:4-3:24. I strongly encourage you to. It won't take long. You got time 😊). In the beginning, Adam and Eve were able to have a close one-on-one relationship with God. Nothing came between them, but there was just one thing that God commanded them to do. He told them they were not to eat the fruit from the Tree of the Knowledge of Good and Evil (Genesis 2:17). The devil was able to persuade them to do it anyway, and this was known as the first sin or the fall of man. Immediately after the fall, Adam and Eve were separated from God. This is because God cannot be associated with sin. He is too holy to be in the presence of it or associated with it. The biggest tragedy is that we were never created to be separated from Him. He never wanted Adam and Eve to know evil, only good! He created us so that we could have a close, intimate relationship with Him (He is supposed to be our first love). Now, because of their rebellion, all their descendants (mankind/all of us) are born with a sin nature. One of the major things we have to suffer with now is a constant battle between our God-given purpose (bringing glory and honor to Him) and our sin nature (our own selfish desires). Something crazy I learned is that the reason the Holy Trinity is able to work together so well is because they have a common goal and never leave the same page. Now, look at us. We were created in God's image, right? Just like there are three Persons in the Godhead, humans have three parts: body, soul, and spirit. Before the fall, they were all working together just fine. But now, since we have this sin nature in us, none of the three parts are working together.

That's where the inner fight comes in. One part of us wants to please our selfish desires, while there is a tug on our spirit telling us that only God can be the source of our joy. We lost sight of our original purpose, which is to live a life that glorifies God and not ourselves. I read somewhere that selfishness was the essence of the fall. Adam and Eve disobeyed God and decided that they wanted to be like God; for this reason, they ate the forbidden fruit. There are a couple other things that came as a result of the fall. I came across an article that describes all of the consequences, and I seriously recommend that you read it. It goes into so much depth and speaks on subjects I never knew were connected with the fall. It blew my mind (Reference: https://bible.org/seriespage/5-fall-man-gods-perfect-plan/ The Fall of Man in God's Perfect Plan).

But here's just a few of them.
- Physical death/old age (Genesis 3:19).
- This is why people lived to be 900 years old in the first couple chapters of Genesis.
- Pain and disease (Genesis 3:16).
- Childbirth pains.
- Loss of innocence.
- Adam and Eve only knew perfection and sinlessness, but after their fall from grace, they immediately experienced guilt and shame for what they had done. This is why they hid from God afterwards.

(Reference: https://answersingenesis.org/blogs/simon-turpin/2016/06/27/five-effects-of-the-fall-in-genesis-3/ Five Effects of the Fall in Genesis 3" Simon Turpin).

God, the Son: Jesus Christ

Do we *need* Jesus to go to Heaven?
Before I go into this, I already know that we don't like hearing about God's judgment. We love hearing about how God is all-loving, but we forget about God's wrath and judgment against sin. You have to know that we cannot go through life living it the way that we want, treating people however we want, living selfishly, and disobeying an all-knowing God's commands. There are consequences (positive and negative) for every single action we take, and sooner or later, those consequences will come back to you (either in this life or in death). And it isn't about God being strict or wanting to hold you back from living your life. The things He commands us not to do are there for our benefit. He wants to protect us from things that could bring us harm, and He is offering something better in its place. Again, it's all about us humbling ourselves and realizing that we don't know it all, nor do we know what is best for us. We know nothing compared to the God who created the entire universe.

Because God is a just God, all sin must be paid for, and the price is death (Romans 6:23: "for the wages of sin is death"). The only way we are able to get into Heaven and have that one-on-one relationship with God is to be without sin. Dr. Tony Evans did an amazing sermon about salvation that has helped me to better understand it. He said that we, as humans, are not able to save ourselves from the punishment of sin. Everyone will and does sin, and God cannot overlook anyone. He described it like this, "Sin created a bill that we couldn't pay." This needed to be said. Because I fell for this lie, too. You cannot get into Heaven just by doing "good" things and living a "good life". I used to believe that just being a person with good morals and values or not doing wrong to anyone was good enough to get you into Heaven or a "better place" when you died. The problem with this is, we are looking at sin as if one is worse than the other. All sin is the same in God's eyes. Although you may not be doing anything horrible like theft or murder, you are still born with a sin nature. All of us commit sin one way or another every single day (lying, cursing, speaking ill about someone, etc.). Let me reference Dr. Tony Evans' sermon again. He said that even though we may be better than some other humans in the way we live (our moral character and how we carry ourselves), it still doesn't meet God's standard to get into Heaven. We would be comparing ourselves to the wrong standard (Romans 3:23: For all have sinned and come short of the glory of God). We cannot meet His standard on our own. We do not have the capability. There is no way we, as humans, are able to truly put our faith on a works system to get into Heaven. Refraining from eating certain foods, speaking certain mantras every day, or doing routines and rituals will not grant us access into Heaven. We are all human, and it is inevitable that we are going to make mistakes. Even when we try our best to live right, we will always slip up every now and then. Faith in Christ alone is the only way to get into Heaven, not faith and works or faith apart from works. If it goes against God's Word, then it is sin. Only Jesus Christ can be our Savior from sin because there is no human born without a sin nature. There is no possible way we can save ourselves because we all sin. So, how does God rectify this situation?

o **TEMPORARY SOLUTION**

For God's people (Jews) to still have a relationship with Him, back in the Old Testament, He created different laws and ceremonies for them to follow (you can read about them in books of Exodus and Leviticus). I know it sounds bad, right? Rules in order to get to God. But because of the fall and their sin nature, they needed to do certain things to understand holiness.

There was a tent where all of these ceremonies would occur called the Tabernacle or "the Tent of Meeting." The High Priest was someone who was chosen specifically by God Himself to represent all of His people. He acted something like a bridge between the people and God, and gave sacrifices on behalf of them. Once a year on Yom Kippur, also known as the Day of Atonement (atonement means reparation for a wrong or injury), the High Priest would enter into a place called the Holy of Holies. The Holy of Holies was the most sacred area of the Tabernacle because it was filled with God's presence. Not just anyone could enter because God could not be that close to sin. In there, he offered the blood of slain animals as a sacrifice on an altar to God; this blood was needed for God to forgive His people of their sins. This sacrifice would only be good until the following year. The animal had to be pure and innocent in order for it to be accepted. There was also a veil that separated the rest of the tent from the Holy of Holies as well. This was symbolic of the separation of God from humanity. But praise God that He came up with a solution that eliminated all of those laws and ceremonies needed to get close to Him (Romans 5:8). But there was a problem.

God, the Son: Jesus Christ

"However, the blood of animals couldn't take away the root cause of the problem, the sin in human nature. After their sins were forgiven, the people continued to sin. To commit sin is to consciously do something that you know goes against God's will. This can be in word, deed, or even thought, (see **James 1:14-15**), meaning that they had to come back and sacrifice again, year after year. Not even the high priest could help them; he himself was a sinner, and the sacrifice was for himself just as much as it was for the people (Hebrews 10:1-4)."
(Reference: https://activechristianity.org/jesus-die-cross)

- o **THE FINAL SOLUTION**

Now, because of Jesus Christ, we are able to have a close relationship with God, the Father. He is the perfect sacrifice and High Priest rolled into one. Let me break it down for you.

- ✓ When Christ died on the cross for us, He became the sacrificial animal needed in earlier ceremonies. He lived a life without sin (pure/innocent). And remember, the animal used for the sacrifice had to be "without blemish". When He hung on the cross on Good Friday, He took on ALL the sins of everyone—past, present, and future. He knew exactly what He was about to endure, and He did it for us anyway! Mark 14:35-36 reads, "He went on a little farther and fell to the ground. He prayed that, if it were possible, the awful hour awaiting him might pass him by. Please take this cup of suffering away from me. Yet I want your will to be done, not mine." He died for each of us individually. He took every single person's sins, knowing exactly who they are and what they'd done. He suffered our punishment so that we wouldn't have to! How remarkable is that?! He gave Himself as the sacrifice we needed! (This is also the only time you see God turn His back on His Son, because God cannot be associated with sin.)

- ✓ Christ acted as our High Priest, because He was specifically chosen by God, the Father. (Hebrews 4:14-16: "Therefore, since we have a great high priest who has gone to heaven, Jesus the Son of God, let us live our lives consistent with our confession of faith. For we do not have a high priest who is unable to sympathize with our weaknesses. Instead, we have one who in every respect has been tempted as we are, yet he never sinned. So, let us keep on coming boldly to the throne of grace, so that we may obtain mercy and find grace to help us in our time of need".) So, when you pray, He serves as the bridge between you and God. This is why at the end of your prayer, you say, "In Jesus' name...."

"One other important point about Jesus' priesthood—every priest is appointed from among men. Jesus, though God from eternity, became a man in order to suffer death and serve as our High Priest" (Hebrews 2:9).
(Reference: https://www.gotquestions.org/Jesus-High-Priest.html/ What Does It Mean That Jesus Is Our High Priest?)

This is why after Christ died on the cross, the veil in the Holy of

Holies tore. And it tore from the top to the bottom, meaning no man had done it! (Matthew 27:51: At that moment the curtain of the temple was torn in two from top to bottom.) God did it to symbolize that because of His Son's death, we didn't have to be separated from Him anymore! HIGH PRIEST, CHECK!

- o **IMPORTANCE OF HIS RESURRECTION**

What makes all of this even more fantastic is that Jesus didn't just die on the cross (Good Friday). The fantastic news is that Jesus is still living because He conquered death and He rose again after being dead for three days (Resurrection/Easter)! This proves His power and authority over all things! It is not possible to have a living and daily faith when you have a dead Savior. 1 Corinthians 15:17 reads, "If Christ has not been raised, your faith is worthless; you are still in your sins". Jesus' resurrection grants you eternal life in Heaven with Him, too. When we accept Christ as our Savior from sin, we now have the power over death as well (eternal life with Him after physical death)! When you get to Heaven, it will be like you never sinned. God will look at the fact that you believe in His Son, and He will overlook all your sins because the wages of sin have been paid for. "Because of the power of the cross, our enemy no longer has any hold on us." (Reference: https://www.gotquestions.org/helmet-of-salvation.html, "What Is The Helmet of Salvation"/Ephesians 6:17?)

He sees that you believe in His Son and forgives your sins. None of us deserve this gift that God has given us. And get this, His power lives in you when you accept Him as your Savior! The same power that raised Him from the dead is in you! No longer are you a slave and in bondage to sin; you are free!!

The enemy could not kill Him! And please do your research and don't take my word for it! I've learned that there are several historical accounts that back up Jesus' resurrection.
Start out by looking at some of these websites:
- https://www.desiringgod.org/articles/historical-evidence-for-the-resurrection
- https://billygraham.org/decision-magazine/april-2011/the-resurrection-myth-or-history/
- Also look at *The Case for Christ: A Journalist's Personal Investigation of the Evidence for Jesus* by Lee Strobel.

QUICK EXPLANATION OF WHAT LED TO HIS CRUCIFIXION

We know how God planned His Son's resurrection out for our benefit, but how did the people surrounding Jesus play their part in God's plan? The Old Testament spoke of Christ's coming numerous times through symbolism (see Isaiah 9:6, 7:14). But the Jewish people of the New Testament believed that The Messiah (anointed or chosen one) would come to save them from their political turmoil or the Roman rule. They didn't think that He would be coming to save them from death and sin. They were expecting a different "kind" of Messiah. In turn, they got mad when Christ claimed to be the Messiah because He wasn't who they thought He was going to be. They didn't want to listen to what He said and didn't believe that He was the Son of God. Even after He proved it through the miracles that He performed and taught about God's laws in a different way than they were used

God, the Son: Jesus Christ

to, they still didn't believe Him. So, who was responsible for putting Christ on the cross?

The Pharisees were a group of religious people who taught Jewish laws. Their job was supposed to be to tell people how they should live in order to please God, but they were making up their own laws instead, and began to think very highly of themselves. They even used the church to cheat people out of their money. When Jesus came around, He really messed with the system they had in place. Jesus taught from the perspective of someone who, not only knows God, the Father, personally, but He taught from the perspective of God. He spoke to them directly from and as God. He used parables (a story that is used to illustrate a moral or spiritual lesson) to teach God's Word. He used a lot of symbolism that the people would be able to understand and relate to (example: planting and sowing seeds). I also heard someone put it this way. As He was preaching, Jesus would reach people who were tired of religion. This is amazing, right? He was trying to tell the people that there was no need for all of the rules that the Pharisees had been putting in place. He reminded them that God was not simply looking for them to do all of the requirements and sacrifices without genuinely seeking an intimate relationship with Him. It was His way of introducing the new way; this way, we would all be able to be with God—no more rules, just accepting Jesus as our Savior! I once heard someone say that the laws and practices that were put into place in the Old Testament were there to show us that we are not able to stop sinning. We aren't perfect; we're always going to mess up because of our sin nature. This is why Jesus came to die on the cross for us. So, we won't

God, the Son: Jesus Christ

have to be in this continuous cycle of sinning, and then, having to offer up a sacrifice to cover those sins every year.

When Jesus discovered how the Pharisees were abusing their authority in the church to get money out of people, He went in, threw tables around and demanded that they stop (Matthew 21:12-13). Soon after, they plotted to kill Jesus for changing everything around and disrupting their order. Please take some time out and read Matthew 27:32-56 for the full story of Jesus' crucifixion. Meditate on everything He had to go through for us. With Him being one hundred percent God, you have to know that He could've stopped all of the things that were being done to Him, but He chose not to. He was scared out of His mind, and prayed to God that there was a way He could avoid being killed, but He went through it for us anyway (Matthew 26:39). Because He loves us, He endured it all to become the sacrifice that we needed. This is the ultimate act of love!

IMPORTANCE AND SIGNIFICANT FACTS ABOUT HIS BIRTH

While I was reading the Bible in the early stages of my salvation, I came across so many things I never knew about Christ that really helped in my relationship with Him. Little things that we often just skim over when reading through the Gospels that can make a difference in how we see Jesus. One of those points was the way He was brought into this world. We all know the Christmas songs and carols about His birth—we've all heard of how He was born in a manger through the virgin, Mary, and all that, but have we ever stopped to really look at how important His birth was? Let's take a look now. Take a second to write down what you know about His birth now.

WHAT DO I KNOW ABOUT CHRIST'S BIRTH? WHAT ARE MY THOUGHTS ON THE SIGNIFICANCE OF HOW HE WAS BORN?

_____
_____
_____
_____
_____
_____
_____
_____
_____

- ✓ **WHY A VIRGIN???** He chose the virgin, Mary, because if Christ had been conceived naturally, He would have been born with a sin nature embedded in Him. He wouldn't and couldn't contain the one hundred percent God part of His being. Instead, the Holy Spirit conceived Jesus Christ in Mary's womb (Luke 1:35).

- ✓ **WHY A MANGER??** If Jesus is the Son of God, you would think that it would have been a very big event that the whole nation would know about—something elaborate that would bring more attention to Himself. I mean we are talking about God, the Father's only begotten Son here! He could've been born into wealth in a huge castle and all that. But instead, God wanted to allow Jesus to be more approachable, so He chose to deliver His Son in a manger. I don't think I'd feel comfortable going to Him if He were born into some rich, royal family in a mansion or something like that. I'd feel unworthy, like I was wasting His time. But God knew exactly what He was doing. He did it this way to show His humility. He wanted to make sure that any and everybody could come to Jesus boldly and confidently, so He made His birth happen in such a humble way. It allows Him to be more approachable and relatable to man. This is just amazing.

OTHER REASONS HE CAME TO US
- ✓ **WHY DID HE LIVE AMONG US??** God, the Father, sent Him so that He could experience every emotion that we face here on Earth. Now, I don't know about you, but this always threw me for a loop. How is it possible that Jesus was able to go through every single emotion that I feel and experience in day-to-day life? How does He know what it feels like to be dumped by a boyfriend, feel stressed out and overwhelmed about work, or have the people you love turn their backs on you? It didn't make any sense to me. But then I discovered the word "empathy". I was confusing empathy with sympathy. Sympathy is when you feel sorry or compassion for someone else without really

knowing what they are going through, but empathy is when you know exactly how that person feels because you've experienced the same emotion. Empathy is when you have been in the other person's shoes. It may not be the exact same situation, but an empathetic person feels the same things that you do. This is how Jesus relates to us. I used to think that Jesus only sympathizes with us, but the fact that He empathizes with us allows for us to have an even more intimate relationship with Him. Just look at some of the things that He went through that we go through.

- Temptation—Was tempted in the desert by Satan after fasting 40 days. (Matthew 4:1-11)
- Betrayal—Judas (Matthew 26:14-16) /Peter denying Him three times. (Luke 22:54-62)
- Fear—in the garden of Gesthiname, the night before He hung on the cross. (Matthew 26:39)
- Loneliness—the night before His death, none of His disciples/friends stayed awake to pray with Him/had to endure the cross on His own. (Matthew 26:36-44)

When you go to Him with any problem, He will be able to feel and understand exactly what you are going through. It is like talking to your best friend. Whatever storm you have in your life right now, know that Jesus experienced it as well. This was a major breakthrough for me when it came to discovering who Jesus Christ is. He knows and understands exactly what you are going through. This blows my mind!

God, the Son: Jesus Christ

- ✓ He came so that we can know God, the Father's character. Most importantly, we're able to see how He thinks, feels and how much He loves and cares for us (Jesus calls us His friends and not His servants when we allow Him to become our Savior (see John 15:15). He didn't just do this by telling people about the Father either. He showed it by who He talked to, associated with, and ministered to. He never left anyone out. He made sure to speak to any and everyone. He demonstrates all of this when we see Him talking and associating with people of different nationalities and genders (Samaritan and Canaanite women), healing the sick, (note: back then, people with certain diseases were quarantined and were not touched or even around others for fear that they may make other people unclean), and we see this when He gave food to thousands of people.

- ✓ He demonstrated how God, the Father, gave His laws (Ten Commandments) through Moses in the Old Testament (Exodus 20), but His kindness and grace comes through God, the Son. Ever wonder why the Old Testament was filled with a bunch of crazy rules? Yeah, that leads back to Christ too. (To the people who have actually read the Old Testament, kudos to you. I know the struggle of reading it). I had no idea that there were so many things that God required His people to do in the Old Testament in order to have a relationship with Him (Leviticus goes through all of the rules, sacrifices, and offerings). Do you want to know why He had them all? For one, to show that we're unable

God, the Son: Jesus Christ

to make it to Heaven on works alone. Like I've mentioned before, we (as humans) don't have the ability to meet God's one requirement to get to Heaven, which is to live a sinless and holy life. The fact that we have a sin nature makes us fall short on all these rules.

- o Christ also sets the example on how to follow these laws and live a righteous life (John 1:16). Now, because Christ already paid the price for us, we won't be punished with eternal separation from God when we mess up trying to live right. You get what I'm saying? Just to make sure that you understand what I'm saying, write down some things about Christ that you've learned just so you can kind of keep track of your growth. I know it took me a while to really understand how God planned this all out and how everything connects.

WHAT I'VE LEARNED ABOUT CHRIST'S DEATH AND RESURRECTION

_____

_____

_____

_____

_____

The coming of Jesus Christ reminds us just how much God, the Father, loves us. He sent His only Son to die and be a sacrifice for us because He knew we wouldn't be able to make it to Heaven on our own. And He is alive right now! He lives so that He is able to guide His flock. In John 10:27, He goes on record saying," My sheep listen to my voice; I know them, and they follow me." Death could not stop Him. The fact that you are able to have a close relationship with someone who is able to conquer death is truly amazing. He is the greatest friend we could ever ask for. He laid down His life for us, and He knows what we go through on a daily basis. You can't get a better BFF than that y'all, let me tell you. He is our High Priest, King, and Prophet all rolled into one! After He was crucified, He told all His disciples that He was going to send help after He ascended into Heaven. You know what that means—we're moving on to the third Person of the Godhead, the Holy Spirit.

GOD, THE HOLY SPIRIT

And now, we get to the third and final Person of the Godhead—the Holy Ghost! In my opinion, this may be the most misunderstood Person of the Trinity. The extent of my knowledge of the Holy Ghost went as far as when people said they "caught the Holy Ghost." And I know I'm not the only one who's heard this common phrase. As I began to get more serious about my walk with God, I would always hear about the importance of the Holy Spirit; this happens especially when you're new to Christianity. I was told that He lives inside of each and every Christian, telling them what to do and where to go. Maybe, you've heard more than me about the Holy Ghost. Write some things down that you already know about Him.

WHAT I KNOW ABOUT THE HOLY GHOST NOW

God, the Holy Spirit

WHO IS HE?
- ✓ Just like the other two Persons of the Holy Trinity, the Holy Ghost is eternal and was there at the beginning of creation. He is known as the "breath of God".
    - o **Genesis 1:2:** The earth was without form and void; and darkness was on the face of the deep, and the Spirit of God was hovering over the face of the waters. Then God said, 'Let there be light;' and there was light.
    - o **Genesis 2:6-7:** And the Lord God formed man of the dust of the ground, and breathed into his nostrils the breath of life; and man became a living being.
- ✓ Spirit of the Lord (2 Corinthians 3:17).
- ✓ He is the Great Comforter (John 14:26). Jesus Christ promised a Comforter to His disciples after He was seated on the right hand of God in Heaven (John 14:16). Just like Jesus comforted the many people He healed and ministered to, the Holy Spirit takes His place here on Earth after Jesus ascended into Heaven.
- ✓ Author of Scripture (2 Peter 1:21). The Holy Spirit was the driving force behind the Bible getting written! He was able to speak to all 40 authors of the Bible over the span of thousands of years in different countries, telling them what to write, and it still came out cohesive and consistent!

SIGNIFICANCE/HIS ROLE
- ✓ The Holy Spirit operates only as God directs Him (Luke

11:13). Since all of God's children are His, even before their birth, the Holy Spirit is always with the believer, even when they have stepped out of the will of God. He is there to lead all believers to the truth and to enable them to know Christ through a new spiritual birth.

- ✓ He convicts us of sin (John 16:7-11). When we are about to do something that goes against what God wants us to do, there is a small voice in the back of our minds telling us not to do this or just a gut feeling that it's not right. I wonder sometimes if people confuse the Holy Spirit with them having a "sixth sense" about things. Listening to the Holy Spirit is very important when you first begin your walk with God (I'll go into detail about how to know when He's speaking to you later on).

- ✓ He will help produce God-like characteristics. He begins to shape and mold you into who God has called you to be. When you begin to let the Holy Spirit lead you on the path God wants you to be, you'll see some changes to your behavior and attitude. You'll feel more joyful, and you will demonstrate g more patience and kindness. These are some of what "the fruits of The Holy Spirit." Here's a complete list of all His fruits (Galatians 5:22-23):
    - love
    - peace
    - kindness
    - gentleness
    - joy

- patience
- goodness
- self-control
- faithfulness

Quick testimony time! I have definitely noticed that, as I began to follow what the Holy Spirit led me to do, things that used to get under my skin didn't anymore (patience). Even though I wasn't where I wanted to be in life and didn't have a lot of material things that I desired, I was content and happy where I was (joy). It was crazy, and to be honest, it scared me a little because I wasn't acting the way that I normally did. I began to want to do little acts of kindness for people who I wouldn't even want to be bothered with. This is all a part of becoming a new creation in Christ (2 Corinthians 5:17: Therefore, if anyone is in Christ, the new creation has come: The old has gone, the new is here!)

- ✓ He gives us strength. When believers are plagued with temptation, impatience, or any other kind of trials, the Holy Spirit will step in, just before you feel like giving up. He's the one who'll throw the towel back in at you when you think you can't go on anymore. Quitting is not an option with the Holy Spirit. He gives you strength you never knew you had. He'll have you thinking to yourself, "How the heck was I able to push myself to do all that?" I can't tell you how many times I wanted to stop writing this book, work on something else for a little bit and just take a break. I would get so tired, frustrated, and overwhelmed that I just wanted to give up. But when I started talking

God, the Holy Spirit

that kind of stuff to myself, something in me would say, "No, just start typing." And when I listened to that voice and started setting small goals for me to achieve, the Holy Ghost would push me even further than that! He keeps you going. Be grateful that we have Him! Whenever you feel yourself getting weak, pray and ask the Holy Ghost for strength. Get to Him first and acknowledge that you need His help. As you begin to leave your old self behind and allow God to change you, it becomes difficult sometimes to let go of past hurts and harmful habits. There will even be times when your faith fluctuates a little. This is when the Holy Ghost steps in! He helps us fight any doubts that may start to creep into our hearts and minds, and He reminds us of who God is (Galatians 5:16-17)!

✓ After Jesus' resurrection and the introduction of the Holy Ghost, He would guide the disciples as they traveled to different countries, preaching the Gospel. He helped them with what to say to people, how to act, where to go and what to do next on their journeys. Acts 20:22 reads, "And now, compelled by the Spirit, I am going to Jerusalem, not knowing what will happen to me there." This is the Apostle Paul speaking about where the Holy Spirit is leading him next to share the Gospel. He does the same for us today. He gives us clarity on which direction we should take next. When you don't know for sure if God told you to do something, the Holy Ghost will make it clear to you. When you begin to go to God first before you make any decisions in your life and allow Him to lead you, He sends the Holy

Spirit to show you where to go next. It is also important to note that the Holy Ghost will not lead you to do anything that goes against the Word of God. You have to learn how to distinguish between the voices of the Holy Spirit and yourself. I know for a fact that there have been a couple times that I can think of offhand where I have mistaken my desires for the voice of the Holy Spirit. He is the best guidance counselor! He won't give you bad or misguided advice. It's coming straight from Jesus!

- ✓ The Holy Spirit gives scripture relevance to your current situations. Have you ever had a scripture just jump out at you when you're reading the Word? It's like a little mental highlighter went over that one passage. Guess who that was? When you're reading God's Word, there will be times when you read a passage once and it doesn't really stand out to you. Then there's going to be another time you'll read it at the exact moment you need it. Or it could be one passage having multiple meanings for you at different times (John 16:13). He fits the scripture right into our lives to help us, warn us, or enlighten us.

- ✓ He guides us in prayer. He is our Intercessor (Romans 8:26). Let's be honest here. If we were to be left on our own with prayer, we would focus mainly on ourselves and what we want. While we are in the middle of praying, He will put someone on our minds and that's Him telling us that we need to be lifting them up in prayer. Even when we don't know how to say what we really want to pray for,

God, the Holy Spirit

He looks at what is on our hearts and will "translate" our prayers for us. Romans 8:26-27 says it this way, "In the same way, the Spirit helps us in our weakness. We do not know what we ought to pray for, but the Spirit himself intercedes for us through wordless groans. And he who searches our hearts knows the mind of the Spirit, because the Spirit intercedes for God's people in accordance with the will of God." In order to discipline myself, I used an alarm on my phone; I set it to go off every hour so that it would remind me to pray all day, every day. You can imagine how quickly I would run out of things to pray for. There were multiple times when I hit these prayer "roadblocks", and after a while, a person or situation that I was facing would pop into my head. That was the Intercessor! Ephesians 6:18 reads, "And pray in the Spirit on all occasions with all kinds of prayers and requests. With this in mind, be alert and always keep on praying for all the Lord's people."

- ✓ The Holy Spirit also acts as your inner worship leader. Whenever you feel a nudge within yourself to get up and lift your hands or shout, don't fight it! That's the Holy Spirit moving you to praise and worship (Philippians 3:3). It won't be for show when it's led by the Holy Spirit. It will be true and authentic worship, which is what God desires and deserves. I'm not even talking about just at church either. I'll be at home doing housework, and I'll just feel compelled to shout, "Thank You, Jesus. Thank You so much!" I would get this feeling deep in my spirit of

God, the Holy Spirit

thankfulness and gratefulness from what seemed to come out of nowhere. It's beautiful.

And we better thank God He did send us some help because the struggle is real out here, folks. Between avoiding temptation and letting go of our old, sinful nature, us Christians got a whole lot going on and we can't afford to be out here lone wolfing it, you know? Come to think of it, we got three people on our side while we out here fighting the enemy. We got it made! So, what do you think? Do you have a clear understanding of who the Godhead is, and a better grasp on each Person of the Godhead? Write down some things that stood out to you about Them.

WHAT SIGNIFICANT THINGS HAVE I LEARNED SO FAR? WHAT HAS STOOD OUT TO ME ABOUT THE TRINITY?

_____

_____

_____

_____

_____

_____

Now, there are some words and phrases that we have all heard throughout the church and when speaking about religion, for example, faith, salvation, and prayer. How well do we really know them? We know the words, but what do they really mean, and do we have the right ideas about them? In the next section of the book, I'm going to tackle some of them and see what we got right and what we got wrong. Since salvation is key in becoming a Christian, let's start with that. And oh my gosh, thanks for making it this far! Keep reading, it gets better—I promise! And if you have anymore questions, please keep note of them. Maybe they'll get answered in a few pages. 😊

SALVATION
You may have already heard of a few of the following phrases...
- receiving salvation.
- being saved.
- accepting Jesus Christ as your personal Savior.

The definition of salvation is "deliverance from harm, ruin, or loss"(Oxford Dictionary).

But what exactly has God delivered and saved us from? How do you receive it? Why is it so important? How do you know when you've truly received it? I had so many questions at the beginning of my walk with God. Let's review what I said about salvation back when we went over God, the Son. Let's see what you can remember about salvation after reading about Jesus— and don't cheat and go back a couple of pages.

God, the Holy Spirit

WHAT DO I REMEMBER ABOUT SALVATION FROM THE JESUS SECTION OF THE BOOK?

QUICK RECAP OF WHAT SALVATION IS

Short and sweet, God sent His only Son to die for our sins so we wouldn't have to take the punishment for them (John 3:16). Flip back a couple of pages so you can give yourself a refresher and get all of the fine details together.

HOW DO YOU RECEIVE SALVATION?

In many churches, I have seen what is known as the ABC's

of salvation (ADMIT—admit that you are sinner, BELIEVE—believe that Christ died on the cross for your sins, CONFESS—confess that Jesus Christ is Lord). I always thought that they make it look and sound so easy to receive salvation. Just say a few words and you're going to Heaven. I had a hard time believing it was that simple. What God has revealed to me is that it doesn't matter what you say out loud. He looks at your heart. The prayer and ABC's are just to express what is taking place in your heart. The prayer and ABC's of salvation that many churches ask you to recite after saying that you want to accept Christ into your life are not what saves you. It's what's happening on the inside. Dr. Tony Evans said, "It is a transfer of trust from yourself to Christ." It is you realizing that you are not able to save yourself, but only God can save you. Realize that He loves you so much that He sent His own Son to die for you. That's why they say "receiving" salvation. You have to "accept" what God, the Father, has offered you!

SIGNS OF TRULY ACCEPTING SALVATION
And How do you know when you are really saved? Look out for some of these changes in yourself:

- your behavior changes (fruits of the Holy Spirit begin to manifest/He lives in you and is making the necessary changes).
    - things you used to like doing, you don't like or don't want to do anymore/your old self begins to die.
- you start to trust God with every part of your life.
- you put Him and His will for your life above your own desires.

God, the Holy Spirit

And check this out—you don't lose salvation when you give into temptation or disobey God. Salvation is a GIFT from God, and it cannot be taken away! Once you accept Jesus into your heart, you will be forever saved from death. Like I've stated before, it is not enough to believe only in God. Even though acknowledging His existence is important, you must believe that He sent His Son to die for you in order to have eternal life. When you deny the existence of Jesus Christ or the fact that He is the Son of God, you are refusing to receive the only way to have an intimate relationship with God, the Father. Jot down some of the things you've learned about salvation now.

What have I learned about salvation from this section and the section on Jesus Christ?

Moving right along—So, I've quoted all these scriptures from the Bible, supporting everything and everyone I mentioned, right? I know you've heard of it, but do you know the importance of it? What's it really about? What is the Bible? Let's take a look...

THE BIBLE

WHAT DO I KNOW ABOUT THE BIBLE NOW? WHAT SCRIPTURES DO I KNOW?

_____

_____

_____

_____

_____

_____

_____

_____

_____

WHAT IS IT?

Let's go over some quick facts about the Bible that you may or may not know already:

- There are 66 books in the Bible.
    - Split into two sections: The Old Testament and The New Testament
- The Bible was written over the span of 1500 years.

The Bible

- The entire book was originally written in three languages on three different continents.
    - Greek, Hebrew, and Aramaic.
    - Asia, Africa, and Europe.

This book is not just any other book that you fill up your bookshelf with. What lies in this book is unfathomable, and I never knew how deep it was until I really began reading and studying its contents. This book is alive! The Bible is God's spoken Word. This is why it is called the Word of God. Second Timothy 3:16 reads, "All Scripture is breathed out by God and profitable for teaching, for reproof, for correction, and for training in righteousness." Matthew 24:35 goes on to say, "Heaven and earth will pass away, but my words will not pass away." It is full of His wisdom and truth. It has become the world's most translated book. Some of the different names of the Bible are:

- The Holy Scriptures.
- Word of God.
- Sword of the Spirit.
- Book of the Law.

HOW WAS IT WRITTEN?

If you read the Bible from cover to cover, it is crazy how connected and in sync it is. God made it so it all flowed together simultaneously. God spoke to the Bible's authors through the Holy Spirit (Author of The Bible) to write exactly what He wanted them to. This is why the Bible is so unified and consistent; it flows so easily and never contradicts itself. You really get a sense of how unchanging and loyal to His Word God is, since this book is His

Logos Word ("Logos is the Greek term translated as "word," "speech," "principle," or "thought." In Greek philosophy, it also referred to a universal, divine reason or the mind of God" (Reference: https://www.gotquestions.org/what-is-the-Logos.html/ What is the Logos?).

WHO WROTE IT?

There are a total of 40 authors who have contributed to the entire Bible, and each book has a different mood and was written at different time periods. Not only are there different authors, but each of them come from different walks of life and have different professions. Peter was a fisherman, Luke was a doctor, and Paul was initially Saul, a Pharisee who killed and persecuted Christians. The Old Testament was written by people who were chosen by God to carry out a special task (also known as prophets). Some of these authors include Moses and David. It was written before the birth of Jesus Christ (B.C. = "Before Christ"). First Romans 15:4 states, "For whatever was written in former days was written for our instruction, that through endurance and through the encouragement of the Scriptures we might have hope." It begins with Genesis and ends with Malachi. The New Testament was written by people who knew Jesus or by people who were under the guidance of those who did know Him. Some of the authors include Paul, Peter, and John. It was written after Christ was born (A.D. = "After Death"). This section begins with Matthew and ends with Revelation.

WHAT IS IT ABOUT?

I know you're probably thinking, "What else could the

Bible be about? It's about God (period)!" Throughout the different time periods and historical events it was written in, every single book of the Bible goes back to the same core message, which is that the forgiveness of sin is found in Jesus Christ alone, and man is not able to save himself from death. The death and resurrection of Jesus is referred to in all books of the Bible. He may not be mentioned by name, but He is spoken of using symbolism and foreshadowing His coming (you see this a lot in Psalms. The author, David, makes a lot of statements that sound almost identical to what Jesus said or went through). The Word was also written to show Christians how to live righteously and obey God's will. There is no need for Google or Alexa. God's got it all written down in His Word for you. 😊

IMPORTANCE

What is so crazy about this book is that, even though it was written thousands of years ago, it can be applied to your life today! It is still relevant! Every single story in the Bible was written to answer any and all questions that you have regarding God, Jesus, and how to live your life to please Him. I never saw the purpose and power behind this book before my walk with God. I just thought it was another plain ole book. Here's what I've learned about its importance:

- ✓ It strengthens your relationship with Christ. It is through His Word that you find out just how much He loves you. You get to know who He is, PLUS, hear what He has to say. I remember seeing a meme on Facebook that said, "Don't say God's been silent when your Bible's been closed." (I'm going to get into how He speaks to you through His Word in a few pages.) Once you have studied the Bible enough to become familiar with God's character, you won't guess or be confused when God tells you to do something. You will recognize His voice with confidence. Besides prayer, His Word is the main way you are able to see what God says about something.

- ✓ It teaches us how to serve God (see Exodus 20:1-17, Matthew 5:27-48, Matthew 16:24). You will learn how to obey God and resist any distraction that the enemy tries to throw at you to disobey God. God also teaches you how to walk through this life, how to present ourselves to the world now that we are followers of Christ, and how to share His Word with others. There are passages that teach you how to use the gifts that God gave you in order to please Him. In short, it teaches us how to be Christians and why God wants us to obey Him and follow His will for our lives.

- ✓ His Word convicts us. While reading scripture, it could strike a chord in you to do better or stop what you've been doing (Hebrews 4:12: For the word of God is alive and active. Sharper than any double-edged sword, it penetrates even to dividing soul and spirit, joints and marrow; it judges the thoughts and attitudes of the heart.) God presented us with His Word to help transform us to be more like Him. It changes us from the inside out. It only takes one line of scripture to really wake us up and realize that what we've been doing isn't the right way (this is with the help of the Holy Spirit like I mentioned before). It's amazing how these passages were written thousands of years ago and still have an effect on people today. The stories could seem so unrelatable to you, but God allows them to speak to your soul and make you reevaluate how you've been living.

- ✓ Reading the Word equips you with strength and wisdom. When you begin to get attacked by the enemy with fear, doubt, or confusion, you have a point of reference on what to do and say to get yourself back on track. The more you study, the more ammunition you get to ward off the enemy. Scriptures will immediately pop into your head when you get scared or don't know what to do when you really dive into God's Word.

- ✓ By reading His Word, you are able to tell what things are truth and what is false. It is the ultimate reference point when searching for the truth. If you ever have a question about anything, the Bible has an answer for it. If you hear something about God from anyone (including pastors on television), always check and see what the Bible says to see if it is accurate. There are a lot of things going on in society right now that are deemed as okay or acceptable, but what the Bible says about it is completely different.

- ✓ Not only is the Word full of stories, prophecies, and wisdom, it is the main way to discover who God really is. Since the Bible is the voice of God, as you read through each story, you will begin to become familiar with His voice and who He is.

✓ The Word uplifts and encourages us.

DOING SOME RESEARCH, STUDY HABITS, AND DISCIPLINE

Okay, so for those of you who have already tried reading your Word, which one of these methods did you use? And don't pretend like you've never done them, either!

- **Method #1:** Start from the very beginning and just read it through.
- **Method #2:** Open to a random page or point and start reading from there.

I know for me, I loved using the second method, especially when I was young. Needless to say, I got nowhere with either of them. As I was reading, it didn't seem like any of the stories would help out a girl who was going to middle or high school. I thought that most of them were for old people. Using that second method, somehow, my hand would always land on a story about some king whose name I couldn't pronounce. And don't even get me started on trying to decipher the King James Version. It takes me back to my high school days of reading Shakespeare. I needed a translator, along with Sparknotes. All this means is that we need to do some research on the Word, get some study habits and begin to discipline ourselves. I heard someone say something along these lines, "The more time and effort you put into God's Word, the more you get out of it." So, how SHOULD we be reading our Bible? Should you keep a journal or use Google? Let me share with you what I learned.

DISCIPLINE YOURSELF

- ✓ Set a schedule for yourself. Make time every day to read and study. It doesn't matter how long, just make the effort to allow God to speak to you through His Word.

- ✓ Keep an open mind. Don't just assume that you won't get anything out of the Word or that it is irrelevant. Walking into Bible study with a closed mind will only leave you confused, missing vital information and advice that God wants to share with you. Say a silent prayer to God before you open your Bible and ask Him to show you something you never knew about yourself, Him, or your relationship with Him. This is what the Bible is for—it was written for Him to educate you. Just be open and make sure to listen to what He has to say.

STUDY HABITS

So, how and where do you start studying?

- ✓ Go slow and pace yourself. Don't try to take on too much at one time. If you do, you may wind up getting yourself frustrated when you don't understand something right away. Starting off small will help build a daily or weekly study regiment. You can start with reading a couple of verses a night and work your way up to a chapter a night. Start at square one and work your way up. The key is to push yourself. Just stay with it and be consistent. Once you start to feel that the regiment you are using is not allowing you to grow spiritually anymore, it is time to change it and go a little deeper. I think everyone has heard of the idea that you have to do something for about a week for it to really stick. It's going to be so crazy when you start to get excited about reading your Word! That's when you know you've made it.

Testimony—If I'm going to be absolutely honest, when I first started reading the Word, I thought it was boring and I wasn't really learning anything. But once I started praying before reading, and once I started being consistent, I became more and more excited to open my Bible. When the time came right before I went to bed to start reading, I would get very excited. I would think to myself, "What am I going to learn tonight? Dad, what are You going to show me that I never knew before?"

- ✓ Read the Bible in different versions. The Bible has a lot of symbolism and various connections throughout its contents that can be easy to miss. Some of its wording is not to be taken literally (a really good example of this is in Revelation). The King James Version (KJV) is said to be the most accurate, but the hardest to understand. So, what I do is I read the KJV first, then the NLT with commentary so I'm able to get some extra information about the passage. This way, I'm still reading the most accurate version while also reading it in a language I can understand. Additionally, I'm getting a little background information at the same time. I remember seeing a post on social media, showing how accurate the most popular translations are. Here it is right here:

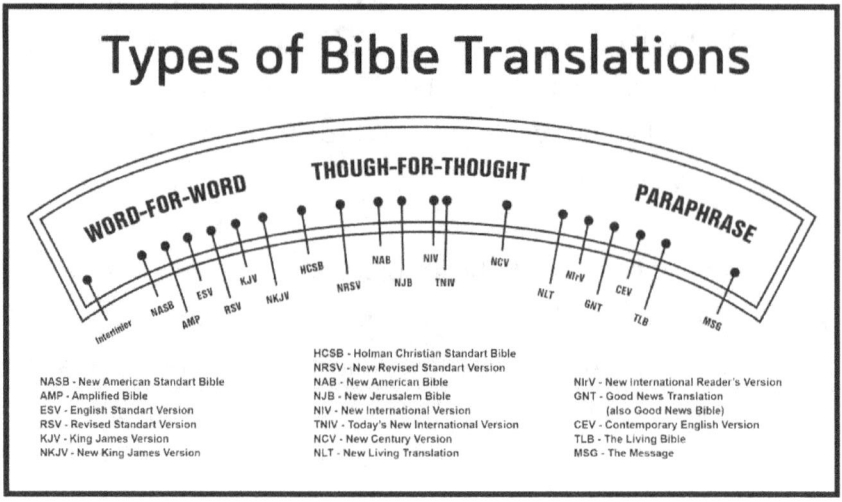

https://agape-house.org/daily-bible-reading-program/

- ✓ Keeping a journal helps as well. Here are some things that you can include in your journal entries:
    - research notes.
    - questions /anything that doesn't make sense to you.
    - verses that stood out to you/meant something to you.
    - what new things you've learned about God, Jesus….

When you keep track of all of these things, it gives you the ability to go back and see how far you have come in your walk with God, the things that He's revealed to you, and to see how faithful He's

The Bible

been to you by answering all the questions you have.

- ✓ Joining a study group can also help answer the questions you have from mature Christians. It will give you different perspectives on Scriptures as well.

RESEARCH

Sometimes, I think we may choose not to read the Word because we don't know where to start and it may seem a little overwhelming. Additionally, when we do pick a place to start, it makes no sense to us. But just because you don't understand something doesn't mean that it's nonsense and that you should just give up. If you do not understand something that the Bible says, first pray on it. Maybe God will lead to start reading a certain book. So, where do you go from there?

- ✓ Let me tell you something. There's no shame in using Google to figure out where to start reading, my friend. USE IT! It's okay to find out which books of the Bible focus on certain topics. Figure out which one tackles a subject that you're struggling with, confused about, or need more knowledge on. Let God lead you to the book that He wants you to read, and then, do your research on it. There are no rules or right/wrong ways to read the Bible. Everyone's method of Bible study and where they begin is going to be different.

- ✓ Ask a mature Christian (elder, minister, Bible study group) where to start.

- ✓ When you begin to dive into studying the Word, it helps to know the who, what, where, and why of the Scriptures you read. Research certain things like the following before reading any book of the Bible:
    - * backstory/why the author wrote it.
    - * time period.
    - * author.

Testimony—When I first got serious about studying the Word, God led me to the Gospels in the New Testament (Matthew, Mark, Luke, and John). Without doing any research beforehand, I would have never known that they all have different styles of writing, they each focus on different aspects of Jesus' life and they appeal to different audiences. For example, Matthew was written to bring attention to Jesus' heritage (Jewish) and His family line throughout the Old Testament. John focused on His deity, as well as Him being human. I also discovered the backstory to certain psalms that matched what I have felt, some of which contained similar situations that I have been in. This helped me to remember that the authors of the Bible have endured the same issues I have, felt the way that I do and that it can be completely relevant to my life! (I'm not telling you how to read the Word, but I suggest starting with the Gospels, particularly the Gospel of John. Out of the four Gospel accounts, John really explains exactly who Jesus Christ is. This book breaks the gospel down and explains it in a way that is so easy to understand. Again, don't take my word for it, ask God where you should start).

HOW TO APPLY IT TO EVERYDAY LIFE

This is the most important step when it comes to reading the Word. You can read the Word and memorize scriptures as much as you want, but unless you apply it to your life, you won't know how to withstand attacks from the enemy, neither will you know how to serve and obey God. It is not enough to just read your occasional devotional. You must really study the Word and digest every single thing that He says in the Bible in order for it to seep into your heart and soul. As you begin to pray and let God lead you through Bible study, the Holy Spirit will often present you with scriptures that will encourage, warn, or guide you — scriptures that fit your current problem or situation. What's also amazing is that He can show you a scripture one day and it has a certain meaning, but He'll show it to you again in the future, and it can have a completely different meaning. You can learn something new that you didn't learn the first time you read it. You have to remember that it is still relevant today. Here are some of the ways you can utilize the Word in your life.

- ✓ Meditation is one of those ways to help you with the application. I didn't really understand what people meant by meditating on the Word of God, because I thought that meditation only applied to New Age techniques. But the way that you meditate on the Word of God is by just pondering and thinking deeply about its different passages. The word meditate means to "think deeply or focus one's mind for a period of time". It's paying close attention to what God is saying in the passage. Take it one word at a time. Use a dictionary if you have to. Meditating

on the Word of God allows it to "dwell in you" and become a source of wisdom (see Colossians 3:16, Joshua 1:8).
- o Make them personal to you and your life. It involves asking, "What is God telling me through this scripture?" or "How does this apply to my life right now?" As you begin to answer these questions, pray and ask God for wisdom and clarity on how the Bible's scriptures relate to your current situation. God will answer if you ask, so don't hesitate!

✓ Memorize any Scripture that has really healed you or encouraged you so that you can bring it up in a moment of need.

Granted, I know that this takes a lot of work, but it'll be worth it when you start to understand the language of the Word and get into the groove of things! Trust me. As time goes on, you will find yourself, not only understanding the Bible's language, but also getting to know God better. When you really start to dig deep in the Word, as well as reading and studying it, it will open up so many more doors of understanding the meaning behind each passage. It is so beautifully written, I just can't explain how amazing it is reading it. I thank God He wrote it for us!

So, if the Bible is one of the main ways God speaks to you, how do you speak to Him? Through prayer, you are able to voice your concerns, fears, and desires. Before we jump into prayer, write some stuff down about the Bible that you've learned or

The Bible

where you think you may start your studying.

<u>What have I learned about the Bible?</u>
<u>Where would I want to start reading?</u>
<u>What am I interested in reading about?</u>

PRAYER

What do I know about prayer now?
Do I believe it's important? Do I think God listens to prayer?

WHAT IS IT?

Prayer is the way that we speak to God. And remember, it's all because of Jesus Christ acting as our High Priest (John 14:6). In each Gospel account in the Bible, the writers made it clear that Jesus prayed consistently. He shows us that in order to maintain a strong and intimate relationship with God, the Father, we must remain in constant communication with Him.

IMPORTANCE

One of the reasons for its importance is prayer gives you the opportunity to confess your sins. When you do this, you are telling God that you realize you have made a mistake and had a moment when you turned away from Him. It gives you the chance for God to show you your error and fix it. The word repent means to "feel or express sincere regret or remorse about one's wrongdoing or sin" (Source: Dictionary.com).

Prayer also humbles you before the Lord. Humility is "a modest or low view of one's own importance; humbleness" (Source: Dictionary.com). When you come to God with your prayers, you acknowledge the fact that you know you need His help and guidance. You recognize who is in true control and you are letting go of your pride.

HOW DO YOU PRAY? DIFFERENT METHODS/"HOW TO'S"

Do I pray now? How do I pray?
Is there a right and wrong way to pray?

I used to believe that there was a certain way you had to pray. You had to come to God only on your knees, eyes closed while saying a whole bunch of big religious words. When I gave my life back to Him, I realized that if I was going to get closer to God, I had to change my views on prayer and try something that I had never tried before. What I have learned is that prayer can be done in many ways. The only thing God tells us all to do is pray constantly! Just like Jesus did, He always took time out to be by Himself to pray to the Father. Being consistent and praying daily maintains the intimacy with you and God.

What are the different ways you can approach prayer? Let me start with what Jesus said about prayer in the Word. When His disciples asked Him how to pray, He gave them an example by saying what is known as the Lord's Prayer. As a side note, the definition of the word "amen" is "so be it".

Matthew 6:9-13:
Our Father, who art in heaven,
Hallowed be thy Name,
Thy kingdom come,
Thy will be done,
On earth as it is in heaven.
Give us this day our daily bread.

**And forgive us our trespasses,
As we forgive those
Who trespass against us.
And lead us not into temptation,
But deliver us from evil.
For thine is the kingdom,
And the power, and the glory,
For ever and ever. Amen.**

This is a blueprint or rough draft of how we should pray and what we should pray for. You start off with the things that are included in the Lord's Prayer, and then, you begin to add the things that are on your heart that come from the Holy Spirit. You don't have to recite it word for word. God is not concerned with you saying the same things over and over again just because you feel like you have to, especially when there is no feeling behind what you are saying. He's not looking for routine prayers just for you to check off your to-do list. He wants to hear directly from your heart.

How to strengthen your prayer life

- ✓ One of the most important things to start off with is to allow the Holy Spirit to lead you when you pray. Like I mentioned before, the Holy Ghost will put on your heart what and who to pray for. While praying, someone or a certain situation may come to mind that seems to be out of nowhere. This is the Spirit of God telling you what to pray for next.

- ✓ Keep a prayer journal. It can be a way to document when

God answerers your prayers, your growth and your maturity, as well as what He reveals to you. When I began writing down my prayers, I would be completely honest with God and bare my whole soul to Him. I began to notice that God would answer my prayers as I was writing them out. It has really helped me remember how faithful God has been to me. When I'm in a tough spot, I just flip back a couple of pages and remind myself of what He has brought me through.

- ✓ Use apps on your phone or use an alarm to remind yourself to pray throughout the day. I have one on my phone set to go off every hour. No matter where I am or if my eyes are closed or open—it doesn't matter if I'm at work, home or running errands, if I feel compelled to speak to Him, I do.

- ✓ Talk to Him like He is a close friend. Go to Him FIRST with any questions, concerns, or problems you may have. This paves the way for God to show you that He will give you strength and courage when you cry out to Him.

Testimony: In the beginning of my walk with God, it was pretty challenging to go to Him first. I had to force myself to go to God before going to anyone else. I was still in the early stages of giving Him my complete trust, so I would still seek out other avenues of advice before going to Him. After I got used to going to God first, the Holy Spirit then guided me in filtering what I said to my friends and family. A lot of times, God has comforted me and calmed me down in a way other people wouldn't be able to do. John 14:27 reads, "Peace I leave with you; my peace I give you. I do not give to you as the world gives. Do not let your hearts be troubled and do not be afraid." If I were to go to anyone else, it may have caused me to get upset all over again. He would give me peace immediately after praying about it.

- ✓ Don't limit your prayer to "normal stuff". Don't just recite the same prayers over and over again, if there is no feeling and thought behind them. Really think about what you are speaking to Him about. Open yourself up to Him. Go into details and specifics. Tell Him ALL of the dirty details! No matter what they are, He wants to hear them. He already knows what you are going through anyway. All of the small everyday prayers that you tell Him will slowly help you to trust Him with the big things that you are concerned about.

Testimony: I realized that it was okay to tell God when I am feeling bad or upset. Because of my view of Him, I never thought that He wanted to hear how I REALLY felt, especially all of my negative thoughts or feelings. I didn't think that I could be that open and honest with Him. But if I was ever dreading going to work or nervous about something in particular, I would make sure to speak on it. I even began to tell Him when I was disappointed with something He'd removed from my life or a command that He wanted me to obey. It makes the relationship more intimate.

- ✓ Call Him Father. It helps you to remember that you are

Prayer

speaking to your true, eternal Father. Like I've said before, He wants to have a relationship with you like a biological father would want to with his child. Just wake up every morning and say, "Morning, Dad!" It makes a world of difference in how you talk to Him AND to know that He's right there with you when you wake up! It's so comforting.

- ✓ Keep praying until you receive an answer. Continue to go to God with all of your issues. First Thessalonians 5:17 says to "pray without ceasing". He won't get annoyed with you if you pray for the same thing over and over again. Even though He is all-knowing, it doesn't mean that it is a waste of time if you go to Him with all of your problems. When you do go to Him, it will allow you to create a dialogue with Him, instead of a monologue.
    - o Don't give up if you don't get an answer right away. Sometimes, God will answer your prayer right away, while at other times, He may take a little while to answer. There is always a reason for His timing. This doesn't mean that He's not listening. He won't have you waiting forever; trust me! He will work on your behalf in HIS perfect timing.

Testimony: While learning how to pray, I remember one time in particular I needed God's healing with letting go of past hurts. I knew that I couldn't get over those hurts with my own strength, so I kept praying and believing that I would soon receive my healing. One night, I was getting very frustrated that I just couldn't rid myself of the pain, so I prayed intensely. I was crying and pleading with God to remove the pain. In that very instant, I felt a huge weight lift off my shoulders and I knew right then and there that I'd received my breakthrough. I trusted God with it (faith) as I was praying, and He gave me my healing! Just keep praying.

HIS DIFFERENT ANSWERS
God has three answers to your prayers:
- Yes
- No
- Not yet (Yes, but wait)

I know some of those answers we may not want to hear at the time, but trust God that there is a reason for the delay or the denial. Remember that God knows what you need and when you need it. Just trust in His timing! Keep the faith and know that He knows what He's doing!

HOW TO KNOW WHEN HE ANSWERS
First things first, you have to make sure that you're hearing the right voice (I will touch on the three different voices later). The key to knowing the difference between them all is getting to know Him. You do this by reading His Word. You're going to have times where you'll be ready to swear that you heard Him say something, and it will turn out to not be Him at all; this is especially true in the early stages of your walk with God. This is because you're still getting to know Him! It is hard to recognize the voice of someone you don't know that well. Over time, as you grow a closer relationship with God, you will be able to know for

sure when He is speaking to you. It is not something that happens overnight, but you MUST find time to listen! I cannot stress this enough. Find a quiet place, uninterrupted by anything or anyone, and just listen. Make time every single day for God to speak to you.

Testimony: I'm going to be completely honest. Early in my walk with Christ, and even until this day, I tend to overthink when it comes to differentiating between the different voices. I don't want to disappoint or disobey Him, so I really want to make sure that I'm getting it right. I've had to accept the fact that I'm not going to get it right all of the time. As time goes on, you're going to get better at pinpointing when the Lord tells you something.

- ✓ You have peace immediately afterwards. Once God has said something to you, a strong sense of confidence and peace will wash over you. God is not a God of confusion (1 Corinthians 14:33), so He will not tell you something that will leave you guessing. You will feel it deep down in your spirit. You'll have security and confidence in what He has just told you. (This is why it is so important to read your Bible and get to know God's character.)

- ✓ It won't go against the Bible. He won't say anything that will contradict Himself.

- ✓ When He tells you to do something, it will either point back to Him or it will be for the benefit of other people. Meaning, whatever He says will give Him the glory. If it is something that is centered around you only, it might not be from Him.

Don't underestimate the power of prayer. When we are confident that God will answer our prayers and know that God has the power to execute those prayers, this is when we'll see mountains moved and people healed. (James 5:16: Therefore confess your sins to each other and pray for each other so that you may be healed. The prayer of a righteous person is powerful and effective). It's having the confidence in Christ that He will make things happen while getting closer to Him in the process!

It's that time again! Write what you've just learned about prayer!

WHAT HAVE I LEARNED ABOUT PRAYER?

I mentioned before that you must have faith when God says yes or no to your prayers. We hear this word a lot, but how do we know when we are truly walking in faith? What do you think? Write some stuff down about what you think faith is.

Prayer

WHAT DO I KNOW ABOUT FAITH NOW?

FAITH

WHAT IT IS
Dictionary.com's definition of faith is "complete trust or confidence in something or someone."

Hebrews 11:1 reads, "Now faith is confidence in what we hope for and assurance about what we do not see." When it comes to spiritual things, we must walk by faith and not by sight. This can be difficult since we live in a physical world and our day-to-day lives are based on what we see and experience with our five senses. However, everything that is spiritual cannot be seen. We live in a world where people pretty much say, "Show me and I'll believe." God says the exact opposite, "Believe me and I'll show you." If God calls for us to have faith in Him, we need to know what faith is in its entirety.

Faith is also an action and is not based on feelings. There will be times when we don't "feel" like we have any faith, but we have to make the conscious decision that we're going to trust God anyway. Emotions have a funny way of tricking us into thinking one way, when it really isn't that way at all. Don't seek spiritual feelings to reassure you of your faith. There will be times when you don't feel close to God or you begin to doubt Him. Even though you feel a certain way about a situation, for example, you feel like you're never going to make it out of a difficult time in your life, the situation itself is subject to the Word of God and not the other way around. (God is working behind the scenes to get you out of that situation). We can't have our faith rooted in what we can see. Faith is based on the unseen; this is crazy; I know. So, why is it so important to have faith when you have a relationship with God?

IMPORTANCE

Faith is the foundation of a relationship with Christ. I mean, you need faith for one of the most important things about Christianity, and that is to believe that God exists. It is impossible to completely believe in the Holy Trinity off of knowledge alone (this goes back to how He is eternal, but we are not). Hebrews 11:6 states, "And without faith it is impossible to please God, because anyone who comes to him must believe that he exists and that he rewards those who earnestly seek him." Just because you don't feel God is close to you doesn't mean that He isn't.

"Your faith is your spiritual energy."—Joshua Eze (Look him up on Youtube. He is an awesome teacher on the Word and he breaks things down so it can be easily understood). Pretty much, the more faith you have in God, the more energy you have to keep on going, no matter what is going on around you. You get what I'm saying?

Testimony: Following my attempt to take control of my life through the use of New Age techniques like the Law of Attraction, I found it very hard for me put my faith fully in God and not in myself. I'd finally figured out what I wanted (or what I thought I wanted) out of life. For this reason, it was so hard for me to completely give it to someone else and lose that control. It was comforting to know that I'd made the blueprint for my life, but when I had to give it to someone else, it was really scary. Do you understand what I'm saying?

HOW WE DEMONSTRATE OUR FAITH IN GOD
- ✓ TRUST HIM WITH HIS PLAN FOR YOUR LIFE.

    - WHO/WHAT WE'RE CALLED TO BE. Oftentimes, God will give you a vision (your purpose/future life) of where your life can be when you put Him first and make the decision to serve Him. Most of the time, it will probably be something that is out of your comfort zone or a task that you feel you're not qualified to handle. It may be something that requires you to seek Him for courage, confidence, and strength. But know this—God doesn't call the qualified, He qualifies the called. He will shape and mold you into the person He is calling you to be! (2 Corinthians 12:9: But he said to me, "My grace is sufficient for you, for my power is made perfect in weakness." Therefore, I will boast all the more gladly about my weaknesses, so that Christ's power may rest on me).

    - TRUSTING HIM WITH THE PROCESS OF REACHING OUR CALLING. All of us want to know what the next move is when it comes to planning for our futures. We need to know the ABC's of how we are going to get where we are going, however, with God, we have to believe that He will guide and protect us until we reach what we're called to do. (Proverbs 3:5-6: Trust in the LORD with all thine heart; and lean not unto thine own understanding). Know that, even though there seems to be no progress being made to what He has shown you, He will get you there soon enough! (2 Corinthians 5:7: For we live by faith, not by sight).

- There will be times when He tells you to do something that doesn't make any sense or it doesn't line up with what you had in mind (I know I felt that way when He told me to write this book), but He wants you to trust and believe that, in the end, it will be worth it and it will finally make sense to you. (The story of Abraham is an amazing example of faith! Read Genesis 11:27–25:10 and Genesis 22).

✓ TRUST HIM WITH YOUR DESIRES. This may be the hardest thing for us to do. Handing over what we want and strive for, and putting it in God's hands is not easy. Letting go of the idea that we can achieve everything on our own is not easy. The attitude of people nowadays is, "Show me, and then, I'll believe you". God wants the exact opposite. Again, He says, "Believe me and I'll show you." He wants you to take Him for His Word, and watch Him work wonders in your life. Everyone knows this takes great faith, but hey, in the longrun, it's going to be worth it. God will always have a much different, but better plan for your life than the one you had in mind. (Ephesians 3:20: Now to him who is able to do far more abundantly than all that we ask or think, according to the power at work within us). God knows so much more than we do. He knows more about us than we do! He knows what we need and what we want. He wants to be in control to show us that He will give us the desires of our hearts when we put Him first. He wants us to believe that when we allow Him to direct our paths, He is leading us into something good and something that will ultimately bring Him the glory.

Testimony: He has shown me where I could be and what blessing could be coming my way if I will just give up my old ways of thinking, habits, and self-centeredness. It is almost like He kind of dangled my dream life in front of my face, but said, "Oh no, wait a minute. You have a couple of things to do and things you have to change before you can have this." But He is telling me that I have to completely trust Him in order to get what I have been wanting my whole life. Luke 1:37 says, "For with God nothing shall be impossible."

- ✓ TRUST HIM WITH YOUR BREAKTHROUGHS AND HEALINGS. Like I mentioned a couple of pages back, it took a while for me to get healed and freed from some past hurts. It was my faith in God that kept me going. I knew that He wasn't going to let those issues hold me back for much longer. He was going to give me the strength I needed to move forward. And that's exactly what happened. Keep your faith in God that He will give you the strength to overcome whatever obstacles you're facing right now. He's going to get you through!

HOW TO STRENGTHEN YOUR FAITH

- ✓ Pray and read your Bible daily. Recite scriptures out loud that focus on having faith in Christ, and meditate on what it is saying to you.

- ✓ Allow God to lead you in the small things. I'm talking small things like giving you patience to deal with people on your job or getting that one parking spot you want at the supermarket. Yes, that small. I'm telling you, it helps so much in your understanding of how God cares about every single prayer you pray, no matter how small.

- ✓ Stay positive! Focus on the things that God has provided for you, instead of what you don't have. It'll remind you that God is for you, not against you, and you can trust Him.

- ✓ Let go of self-reliance and the need to be in control. Now, I'm not saying you need to depend on everyone else and not do anything for yourself. But what I am saying is we have to let go of the attitude that "I can do it on my own; I don't need any help from anyone." There is no way you can believe that you can do everything on your own without any help and still have complete faith in God to supply all your needs. You're not giving God any room to show you what He can do in your life if you keep trying to be in control of everything. To be honest, we all have that one area in our lives we don't want to hand over to God (for me, it's my love life—or lack thereof). God is asking us to trust Him one hundred percent with every single thing in our lives. He wants us to give Him COMPLETE and total access, from our careers to our love lives, from buying a house to having children. We have to humble ourselves and let go of that need to be in control in order to put our trust in God. By doing so, we are telling God that we trust Him enough that He will take care of all of our needs. A lot of the time, God will send you help through other people too! Stay humble and accept the help.

Testimony: I have lived my whole life wanting to be independent—to figure everything out on my own. It was a little difficult for me to believe that God would lead me down the right path. I'd bring my wants and needs to Him, but not believe that He would provide them for me. I would think that I wouldn't be satisfied with whatever He would give me. So, I always created a backup plan to God's plan or always worried about the "what if's". I also recognized that I had to let go of the mindset of trying to figure out God's plan for me before He let it unfold. I had to remember that He wouldn't have something planned for me that wasn't good for me. He knows what we desire; just trust Him. He can handle and take care of it a lot better than we can.

FAITH AND BLESSINGS

How does having faith work along with God blessing you? I heard someone put it this way— "The size of your faith determines the size of your blessings." He doesn't bless you simply because you're doing a lot of "religious" things like going to church a lot, fasting, and saying big preachy words when you pray. He blesses you when He sees your faith in Him! (Not to say that some of the things previously mentioned won't aid in Him blessing you, you just have to have faith WHILE doing these things. Faith over works!)

Testimony: There was a time when it seemed as if God wasn't sending any kind of blessings my way. I listened to all the convictions the Holy Spirit was giving me. It seemed like I was doing everything right. I had stopped cursing, started tithing, and embarked on a journey of abstinence. I thought that doing all of these things would show Him that I was ready to receive a blessing and that I was serious about getting closer to Him. None of the blessings that I prayed for were in sight, no matter how much I prayed and read His Word. I had to watch as everyone around was being blessed with the things I wanted. Now, I realize that, even though doing all of those things are important, they mean nothing if you don't believe that God will bless you. I needed more faith. I've had this attitude that if I don't expect anything spectacular to come out of something, then I wouldn't get hurt when it wouldn't happen. And since I didn't have very strong faith, my life remained stagnant. As soon as I began to put my faith in Him with small things, I began to see little daily blessings. Most of the time, I wouldn't even have to ask for it, He would just bless me. Things that I didn't even think of asking for, He just gave it to me (see Ephesians 3:20). I'm talking like really small things that shows that He really cares. I would be craving a certain food and someone would bring it home without me asking for it! Look at Jesus!

Folks, the ultimate goal in having complete faith in Christ is this—to believe that God is working everything out for your good even when it doesn't look like it on the surface. I've heard it said that, when it doesn't look like God is doing anything, the moments when He's telling you to just wait, that's when He is doing the most. It is when you cannot see what God is working on that He is putting it all together for you. Our faith is tested and proven in God's silence. He's trying to see if you're going to hold onto the things that He has promised you, even when it seems like He's not there. Whenever it seems like God is silent, God is reminding you to trust in Him and be still (I believe the awesome Shamieka Dean said that, also check her out on Youtube). Your not being able to see how God is working it out is His test to see if you really trust and believe in Him. It doesn't matter if you're in the waiting season or simply trying to build and keep the faith. He will lead you into something good, even though you might encounter some obstacles and unexpected detours along the way. I know a lot of you have seen the meme that says, "The teacher is always quiet during a test". Side note: A lot of times when our faith is being challenged, we tend to blame the enemy. But if we find ourselves constantly getting redirected and thrown off course, it may be us fighting God's will for our lives. We could be trying to hold onto something God is telling us to let go of. Or we could be going against God's time table. Just wanted to add that in there for you 😊.

Testimony: Let me share one more testimony of faith with you. A while ago, I was going to go on vacation with my friend, her family, and my son. When it got closer to the date to leave, I realized that I didn't have a lot of money saved up to spend on extra food, diapers, and souvenirs while I was down there. I began to freak out and fear that I would be on vacation with no money. It would have been so embarrassing. I calmed myself down and just prayed. I started to think of different ways I could get more money and couldn't come up with anything. Then, I remembered that God had allowed me to pay for the trip completely, and He'd allowed for me to get this opportunity, so why would He allow me to get this chance to show my son an awesome time without Him providing me with the extra money that I needed? I prayed, strengthened my faith, and really believed that He would send me the money that I needed. In the days leading up to us leaving, God told me to ask my mother for some extra money. When He told me this, my automatic reaction was a resounding no! I hate asking people, especially my parents, for any kind of help, especially when it comes to money. But I sucked it up, obeyed God and asked my mother if she had any extra money she could loan me until I got back. She said yes and offered it to me with no hesitation. All in the same day, I received about two hundred dollars. Some of my cousins who were visiting from out of town heard that I was going on vacation and gave me money too. That very same day, my grandmother gave me money for the trip and my sister gave me some money that she had owed from a few months before. Once I stopped trying to figure out how I was going to solve my money problem—once I turned it over to God and let Him handle it, everything not only worked out okay, but it turned out ten times better than I thought that it was going to be. Originally, I thought that I was going to go down to Florida with sixty dollars to spend until the other payment was deposited in my account. Instead, I ended up having over two hundred dollars to spend while I was down there.

I'm beginning to learn that God really wants to bless you; you just have to believe it. From tiny everyday occurrences to big life decisions. Just trust Him with it all. Our Father takes good care of His children. One of the key things that you should do while you are waiting, whether it be for a blessing, a breakthrough or for healing is to praise Him. Worship Him for all that He has done for you. But, how do you praise and worship Him? What are the differences between the two? Let's go over them. Write down what you've learned about faith or even your plan to strengthen your faith.

WHAT HAVE I LEARNED ABOUT FAITH? HOW CAN I STRENGTHEN MY FAITH IN CHRIST?

Faith

PRAISE AND WORSHIP

Normally, when you hear the words praise and worship, some of the things that may come to mind are music, dancing, and maybe even running around the church.

Testimony: I've witnessed people throw their hands in the air, stomp their feet, shout and cry, and not just older people either. When I was in middle school, I remember seeing a girl my age jumping up and down, stomping her feet during praise and worship at our church's annual youth retreat. Witnessing this girl who was the same age as me worship the way that she did has stayed with me until this day. I wondered what was going on with her to make her act like that, regardless of the fact that other people were watching her. It baffled me. I used to think that praise and worship were only physical and not spiritual; I thought that they could only be seen. I thought people only did it in front of other people, and it was supposed to be loud and enthusiastic. I just figured that they were doing it for attention or just because everyone else was doing it. So, what exactly is true praise and worship? The first thing that took me by surprise was that there is a significant difference between the two. Did you know that there was a difference? What do you know about each of them?

WHAT DO YOU KNOW ABOUT PRAISE AND WORSHIP NOW? DO YOU THINK THERE IS A DIFFERENCE?

Let me break down praise first.

WHAT IS PRAISE?
  Praise is joyfully recognizing all that God has done for you. It is remembering how faithful He has been to you and how He continues to bless you. When you praise God, you are being thankful. It's an expression of faith and declaration of victory (Reference: https://danielonyegbule.wordpress.com/2015/11/14/praise-is-an-expression-of-faith-and-a-declaration-of-victory/ Praise Is An Expression of Faith and a Declaration of Victory).

"A definition of Christian praise is *the joyful thanking and adoring of God, the celebration of His goodness and grace*" (Reference:

Praise and Worship

https://www.allaboutgod.com/praising-god.htm/ Praising God). It is recognizing that, no matter what your situation looks like, you're happy that He is going to bring you out better than you went in. True praise always comes from the heart! It is not for show!

HOW DO YOU PRAISE?
Like I've said earlier, praise manifests itself in our bodies, so praise can include some of the following things:
- Singing
- Clapping hands
- Stomping feet
- Dancing (praise dancing)
- Prayer (thanking Him for all that He has done)
- Speaking about Him to others
    - Saying scriptures from the book of Psalms out loud (I normally do when I first wake up and before I go to bed).
    - Not only can you praise God directly to Him, you can praise God by telling other people what He has done for you.

Want to know what praise can look like? Let me use a pretty widely known example—We've all either seen it or heard about it—when someone gets "slain in the Spirit" or "catches the Holy Ghost." You see people jumping up and down, shouting, or doing some other enthusiastic motion. I read somewhere that praise manifests itself in our bodies and souls, and this is why people tend to dance and move around because they cannot

Praise and Worship

contain the overwhelming feeling of gratitude that they have towards God. Once you begin to feel and realize how good God has been to you and you just can't hold the joy inside, you enter praise. It's all about completely letting yourself go and just expressing with your whole heart how thankful you are and acknowledging how good God is.

Testimony: There have been numerous times, either at home watching a sermon on television or at church, where my then two-year-old son would raise his hands as if he were saying, "Hallelujah!" Sometimes, it may just be that he's imitating what he's seeing, but I really do believe that he is feeling the Holy Spirit's presence in the room. He would get up on the pew in church during praise and worship, and just start smiling, laughing, clapping his hands and moving along to the music. It is a beautiful sight to see.

IMPORTANCE OF PRAISE

- ✓ It is giving God all the credit for your blessings. Just look at all that He has done for you now and think about what He has planned for you in the future! I mean, He does deserve it; don't you think? You are recognizing and being thankful for His authority, power, and guidance in your life. It takes the focus off of us and reminds us that He is in complete control! It's a way of humbling ourselves!

- ✓ Strengthens your faith. When you begin to reflect on what God has done for you, you start to realize

Praise and Worship

that God will do what says He's going to do.

- ✓ Can stop the enemy from attacking. Whenever you feel attacked by the enemy, get on your knees and start praising Jesus for all that He has done for you. It shuts the enemy up in a heartbeat.

Testimony: A few years ago, I found it so hard for me to let go and just praise God wholeheartedly, for example, doing things like lifting my hands, singing along with the choir, just really showing it outwardly—you get my point. I was so worried about how I would look to other people. I didn't want them thinking that I was being fake, you know? But let me tell you how I got over it. It started with me refusing to allow myself to hold back my tears if I was overcome with emotion (which happens every Sunday at church, mind you). After this, I began clapping when I understood the pastor's points in the sermon. Next, it went to me nodding my head, and eventually, standing up and clapping. The more and more I did, the more steps I took, the more comfortable I became with doing whatever the Holy Spirit led me to do. And this was just at church. I still had the problem of doing it at home as well. I still thought about how I would look while I was praising Him. But again, it started with doing small things first. It would start with me getting on my knees and saying, "Thank you." I'm not even talking about for big stuff, it would be little everyday things, and it would just grow from there. As I practiced this more, I would get random moments when I would just break out in praise. Two years later, I have no fear and don't hold back from giving Him the praise that He deserves. I don't care what other people think

Praise and Worship

while I'm doing it, and I don't need music, nor do I need to listen to a sermon. When I began to get more comfortable praising Him in front of other people, I noticed that the second after I started, I would get these nagging thoughts in the back of my mind. I would hear, "You look so weird" or "People will think that you're crazy." I would also hear, "Why would you lift your hands like that?" It was endless. I know that if I continue with this process, I will reach the point where I will be shouting praises out loud in front of others! Pray for me. Seriously. Don't let the enemy try and stop you from giving God praise for fear of what people will say about you. Lift up your hands and shout out loud. He deserves it! Be encouraged.

Now, that we know what praise is, worship is next in line.

WHAT IS WORSHIP?

To start off, worship is kind of like praise in that it is based on what God has done for you. You are still showing your gratefulness and giving Him all of the credit for everything. But this is where they differ. It is a little more difficult to do compared to praise. Praise can be given to anyone without any major effort or sacrifice. You can give anyone praise, be it your coworker, friend, or child. It doesn't require anything of you to praise someone. You are letting God know that you are putting Him in complete control of your life. You acknowledge that you are putting nothing before Him and your relationship with Him. Obeying His commands and serving Him is the most important thing in your life. Worship occurs at a much deeper level than praise. It happens in our innermost being or our spirit (John 4:24: God *is* Spirit, and those who worship Him must worship in spirit and truth.")

What shocked me when I was learning about worship was that it is actually a lifestyle (Romans 12:1-2)! Yeah, I know, right? I didn't think you had to engrain it in your day-to-day life. Romans 12:1-2 says to "present your body as a living sacrifice," meaning, everything about you (mind, body, soul) must be submitted to God to be called worship. It is a continuous and daily act. A worshipping lifestyle includes:
- Reading the Bible
- Praying
- Fasting
- Serving others

IMPORTANCE OF WORSHIP
- ✓ Giving Him worship will bring you closer to Him. Worship is relational (Reference: https://relevantmagazine.com/god/worship/features/25684-whats-the-point-of-worship). This goes back to how God wants to be first in your life and know you at the most intimate level possible. When you worship, because it comes from deep within your spirit, you are telling Him that you put Him first in your life! You let go of pride, ego, and self-worship.

- ✓ Makes certain that you're not putting anything else before Him. Worship is something that must be reserved for God ONLY! One way or another, we are all worshipping something. Be it money, ourselves, health, marriage, etc.

Whatever you choose to worship becomes your all—the thing you put faith in. You need something solid and unshakable to surrender to—something that is unshakable. When you don't worship God, you are worshipping something or someone else. This is why God looks at your heart and not what you are just doing physically. You can look like you are praising Him while you are worshipping something else. Make sure you are worshipping the right thing!

Side note: whatever we worship says a whole lot about how we think and feel.

HOW DO YOU WORSHIP?

This is how you know when you're worshipping God:

- ✓ Your lifestyle.
    - o Take a look at the things I listed a few pages ago.

- ✓ You put nothing else before God in your life. You seek Him first, put your faith in Him, and rely on only Him for strength and fulfillment.

- ✓ You have a desire to please and obey God.

    - o Includes bowing and kneeling. This is because you are showing complete surrender to God (Reference: https://www.gotquestions.org/difference-praise-worship.html/ What Is The Difference Between

Praise and Worship?). But again, worship is about the heart, not necessarily what is shown on the outside.

Testimony: As I got better with praising Him, worshipping Him came right behind it. I *wanted* to worship Him because I knew that it pleases Him and it would bring me closer to Him. I made the decision to try and "practice" worshipping Him. It started with me worshipping Him in the car. There would be times when I sang Gospel songs and would get so caught up that I began to cry and praise Him right then and there. Then, it went to doing it at home alone in my room. If a thought or feeling of gratitude came to me, I would just say a silent prayer of praise and humility for a couple of minutes. Nothing will hinder me from worshipping and praising Jesus in public. With each step I take, I experience a new level of God's presence that I have never experienced before. It allows me to see a new "side" of Him.

As an added bonus fact: You know how in church, they play two different kinds of music for praise and worship? For the people who only been to church once or twice (no judgment 😊), let me school you. Normally, the choir or praise team will sing lively, upbeat songs, and then, slower, more…." serious" songs. This is to encourage both praise AND worship!

Both praise and worship are more than music, dancing, kneeling, and bowing. They are rooted in showing gratitude for what God has done for you; they are submitting ourselves to Him and humbling ourselves before Him, in our hearts and our lifestyles. Don't be scared to do it in front of others. You may just encourage someone around you to let go as well. What did you take away from this discussion on praise and worship?

WHAT DID I LEARN ABOUT PRAISE AND WORSHIP?

Now, how can we incorporate all of these things into our daily lives? When you decide to give your life over to Christ (if you haven't already), what comes next? How are we to live in a world that goes completely against what God is calling us to do? How do we transition from our "worldly" selves to our "Godly" selves? Let's figure it out. Write down anything that stuck out to you from this last section.

WHAT HAVE I LEARNED ABOUT THE BIBLE, FAITH, SALVATION, PRAISE AND WORSHIP?

HOW GOD CHANGES AND SANCTIFIES YOU/WHAT DOES IT LOOK LIKE

It seriously made me very nervous to know that I was going to have to give up some of the things I used to do before Christ. I assumed that I was going to live a miserable life and not have any more fun. I mean, no more drinking, cussing, going wherever I wanted—I just thought it couldn't get any better than I had it when I was in the world. Sometimes, I just have to laugh at that thought. How about you? What comes to mind when you think of God changing you? Are you scared, excited, nervous or nauseous?

WHAT ARE YOUR THOUGHTS ON GOD CHANGING YOU AFTER RECEIVING SALVATION? DO YOU THINK IT'S NECESSARY?

Now, before you get too scared, just remember that God is a God of restoration. Whatever He tells you to give up, He will replace it with something ten times better. He'll have you forgetting you ever wanted, needed, and liked whatever it was that you had to sacrifice. Trust me, I know from experience. He has restored so many things in my life, and I am not trying to go back to the lifestyle I had before I knew Him. I've heard someone say, "Instead of looking at the pain of the past and present, look at the favor of the future." And please know this—when God tells you to let go of something, He isn't telling you to do it using your own strength (let that sink in a minute). He knows that eventually, you are going to trip up or get tempted to backtrack. He knows how hard it's going to be to leave the past behind, especially when everything in you is telling you not to. But you're not alone, and He's not telling you to handle it on your own. You have to rely on Him as your source of strength and love. We CANNOT do it on our own! His strength is made perfect in our weakness (see 2 Corinthians 12:9)! Okay, now that I've gotten that out of the way, I'm going to go through some of the things that God will begin to change in you and what He will ask you to get rid of. After this, I'll talk about some of the ways God gives you to help aid in the transition, and some of the things that helped me in the transition. Now, I'm not saying that it's going to be the same for every single Christian, for example, He does tell us to stop watching certain movies or television shows, but these are just some common ones. Each transition is going to be different.

WHAT YOU WILL HAVE TO CHANGE OR GET RID OF
- ✓ Bad attitude/mindset

- o It could be your attitude towards other people, yourself, relationships, or anything and everything. I cannot tell you how many things He has revealed and continues to reveal to me about my attitude.
- ✓ Likes/dislikes
    - o Types of movies, music, hobbies, books, television shows, clothes
- ✓ Views/opinions
    - o Social/ global issues
        - Homosexuality, abortion, etc.
    - o Politics
    - o Religion
    - o Sex/love/relationships
    - o Opposite sex
    - o Yourself/self esteem
- ✓ Hanging around certain people
    - o Friends or family. As hard as it would be, for some people, it may have to come to this. You cannot move forward with Christ if you're going to be hanging around people who enable the behavior that He is telling you to stop. It may get a little lonely, but it's better to be alone with Christ than to battle back and forth between your old ways and His ways.
- ✓ Occupation/career choice

HOW TO KNOW IF YOU'RE CHANGING

Want to know if He's beginning to change you or not?

- ✓ Conviction. When you mess up and do something that God is commanding you not to do, how do you feel afterward, or even while you're doing it? Do you feel some discomfort or a little nudge in your spirit, telling you that you shouldn't be doing it; if so, guess what? That's God changing you. In other words, He's convicting you. Conviction is somewhat like a deep sorrow and nagging feeling that what you're doing is wrong. It's the Holy Spirit telling you that what you're doing is displeasing and upsetting to God. It's what leads us to asking God for forgiveness and not wanting to make the same mistakes again. "Conviction is the work of the Holy Spirit where a person is able to see himself as God sees him: guilty, defiled, and totally unable to save himself (John 16:8). Conviction functions differently for the Christian and non-Christian. For the non-Christian, conviction reveals sinfulness, guilt and brings fear of God's righteous judgment. Whereas, conviction in the believer brings an awareness of sin and results in repentance, confession and cleansing" (Reference: https://carm.org/dictionary-conviction).

Testimony: I went to a club a couple of months after deciding to put God first in my life. All the way there, something in me was saying, "You shouldn't go, you shouldn't go." It just didn't feel right, but me being stubborn, I went anyway. I had a pretty good time, too. It was the next morning that did me in. Not only was I slightly hungover, I felt very guilty and ashamed. I can't stress to you how important it is that you don't ignore those feelings of discomfort, which is called grieving the Holy Spirit. There is always a reason why He is telling you to let those things go. When you make the conscious decision to obey Him and let go of those things, He'll replace what you gave up with something much better. He'll even take it a step further and explain to you why you need to let it go. So, don't think He's going to just leave you in the dark about why you're giving something up (but it's also not an excuse to disobey Him, even if He doesn't tell you the reason). He'll let you know—in HIS time. He's shown me my motives for going to clubs and bars AFTER I obeyed Him and stopped going. And if you're wondering if you should stop doing something that isn't clearly addressed in the Bible (clubbing, masturbation...), use a simple formula—would my Father like it? Do I feel like I have to hide this? Does it bring God glory? Using these questions will definitely help you.

- ✓ God will eliminate the desire to sin. I noticed that after a couple of months of not drinking and going to clubs, just the smell of alcohol would make me nauseous. Nowadays, just the thought of me drinking enough to where I'm not in complete control of my actions terrifies me. The reason is two-fold—I don't want to put a bad image of Christians out there and I don't want to embarrass my Dad. Your desires will change once you begin to live for Him. You'll want to please Him more than you'll want to please yourself. You'll think about how your actions will affect the body of Christ. And even if you do slip up and do something that God told you not to do, He will make you feel so uncomfortable and convicted that you won't want to do it again!

Again, He'll replace things that He asks you to sacrifice to follow Him. Let me go through a list of what He gives you.
- Peace of mind
- Joy, especially in the littlest things
- Purpose/calling
    - Discovering what cross God is asking you to bear. "Your cross is the thing you must die on in order for someone else to live." —Joshua Eze
    - You have to take this time to allow God to show you who you really are. Not the different personality traits and strongholds you've picked up from your hurts and disappointments. Gotta know the "new" you—more like the you that you were supposed to be all along!
        - Self-confidence and esteem through Him
- Other hobbies/ways to have fun
    - Trust me, drinking and clubbing are not the only ways to have fun.
    - This ties into your calling as well. You'll be spending too much time working towards your purpose to be backtracking.

I know I'm probably missing a whole lot, but these are first things that come to mind. Don't let the world get you to thinking that being a Christian requires so much of you and you get nothing in return. God will restore all of the things the enemy took from you while you were living in the world! And the only thing you have to do is trust and obey Him. Give Him that desire to drink, to have sex outside of marriage, to do drugs—whatever it is, and He'll give you His love, peace, and strength in return! GIVING UP WHAT HE'S TELLING YOU TO IS WORTH IT EVERY SINGLE TIME!

During this season, don't be too hard on yourself. This is going to be a really tough time in your life. You're trying not to disobey God, and at the same time, you're letting go of things that you have been used to doing for a long time. You are leaving behind old lifestyles, habits, and thought patterns that you may have had your whole life. You're trying to differentiate between the voices you hear— whether they be yours, God's or the enemy's. (Just a quick reminder: I remember hearing Shameika Dean say this, "If you want to know if God is speaking to you, get your prayer life in order!" Getting to know His voice is done through prayer and reading His Word.) There's going to be times of confusion, wavering faith and doubt. Think of it as having growing pains. Everything about you is being changed and sanctified by God. It will be uncomfortable, and this is why you must go to God for strength, comfort, and encouragement. One of the amazing Joshua Eze's phrases that he says a lot has stuck with me and helped me so much that I have it written on my pinboard in my room. He said, "PROGRESS, NOT PERFECTION". As long as you're doing better than you were the day before, that's all that matters. Take it one day at a time...

THE ENEMY'S ROLE IN THE TRANSITION
I think it's about time to introduce who we're going up

Praise and Worship

against. The enemy's (Satan/the devil) major plan is to try and keep you stuck in your ways so your testimony becomes ineffective and you give a bad representation of Christians. Satan will attack you with doubt ("Did God really say...?" or "Will it really hurt you if...?"). He'll even get you with the "what if's" ("What if God doesn't come through?" or "What if you're wrong about this?"), coupled with negative thoughts. He wants you stuck in those old mindsets and habits, holding onto unforgiveness and bitterness. He wants you harboring jealousy in your heart and continuing generational curses. I mean, think about it. How much of an impact would Christians make if we got saved and then didn't change to become like Christ? We wouldn't really be showing God's joy and peace to other people if we're walking around still doing the same things we did before we got saved.

Testimony: I struggled with letting go of bars and clubs a lot within the first two years of me giving my life back to my Christ. The enemy would constantly have me going back and forth, telling me, "God didn't really say that. He didn't say you couldn't go *here*. Other Christians do it, too; so what?" I thought I was losing my mind at times because I kept going back and forth in my head and fighting against what I really wanted to do. It was hard, but with discipline, God's strength in me and by me staying focused, I was able to block out the enemy's attempts to sabotage my obedience to the Father.

It's an ongoing invisible fight within yourself and within your spirit. It's all done in the mind because that's just what the enemy is after! I'm going to tell you what God has given us to fight the enemy off! He doesn't leave us unprepared!

GOD GIVES US SYSTEMS AND METHODS TO GET THROUGH THE TRANSITION

The enemy can be very subtle and sneaky when he tempts you, so don't underestimate him! He'll use ANYONE to make you question your walk, and do whatever it takes to weaken your relationship with Christ. Remember that invisible fight I told you about a couple of pages ago? (1 Peter 5:8: Be alert and of sober mind. Your enemy the devil prowls around like a roaring lion looking for someone to devour.) But, don't fret, because our Dad always takes care of His kids! Along with the Holy Spirit, He has equipped us with something that will deflect the attacks of the enemy every single time! Introducing— THE FULL ARMOR OF GOD! Have you heard about the armor of God? What do you know about the armor now?

WHAT DO I KNOW ABOUT THE FULL ARMOR OF GOD NOW?

WHAT IS THE FULL ARMOR OF GOD?
- ✓ We see the armor of God in Ephesians 6: 11-17 when Paul, the author of Ephesians, breaks down each piece. Ephesians 6:11 reads, "Put on the full armor of God, so that you can take your stand against the devil's schemes."

- ✓ There are six pieces that make up the armor:
  - Belt of truth
  - Breastplate of righteousness
  - Shoes of preparation
  - Shield of faith
  - Helmet of salvation
  - Sword of the Spirit

IMPORTANCE OF ARMOR

Ephesians 6:12 says, "For we do not wrestle against flesh and blood, but against principalities, against powers, against the rulers of the darkness of this age, [a] against spiritual hosts of wickedness in the heavenly places." Our true battle isn't in the physical (what we can see, touch, hear, smell or taste). If you really look at it for what it is, we're not battling other people, our finances, or anything like that. What we are fighting is a reflection of what's going on in the spirit world (heard that from Joshua Eze as well). We need to strengthen our spirit man if we are going to win this fight. Now, let's get into each one of these pieces of the armor. Just to help with a little visualization, picture a Roman soldier as we go through each piece of armor. (Note: Ephesians was written during the time of the Romans.) Imagine someone from 300 or Troy. Up first, the belt of truth!

BELT OF TRUTH (EPHESIANS 6:14)

WHY WOULD TRUTH BE REPRESENTED BY A BELT?

WHY IS TRUTH A BELT?

PHYSICAL

It holds all the other pieces of armor together! The belt of a Roman soldier in Paul's day was not a simple leather strap such as we wear today. "It was a thick, heavy leather and metal band with a protective piece hanging down from the front of it. The belt held the soldier's sword and other weapons" (Reference: https://www.gotquestions.org/belt-of-truth.html/ What is The Belt of Truth/Ephesians 6:14?).

SPIRITUAL

What truth is Paul referring to? It's all of God's promises, commands/commandments. It's His Word (the Bible, better yet, the Sword of the Spirit, which the belt of truth also holds!) Do you see a connection here? Without God's truth, we are lost and confused. We would be swayed to and from, believe and follow every opinion thrown at us, and accept all the lies and deceptions the enemy uses to ensnare us. It's His truth that holds everything together.

It could also be referencing Jesus Christ. He said in John 14:6, "I am the way, THE TRUTH, and the life. No one comes to the Father except through Me."

HOW DO YOU PUT ON THE BELT OF TRUTH??
- ✓ Fill your mind and meditate on the promises that God has given you through His Word (He will always be with you, He has given you a spirit of power, love, and self-discipline). What this will do is ground you In God's truth (sturdy, strong, unmovable), instead of the enemy's lies (shaky, weak, unreliable).

- ✓ Remind yourself who Jesus is and that His power lives in you!

BREASTPLATE OF RIGHTEOUSNESS (Ephesians 6:14)

<u>**WHY WOULD RIGHTEOUSNESS BE REPRESENTED BY A BREASTPLATE? WHAT DOES RIGHTEOUSNESS MEAN?**</u>

WHAT IS RIGHTEOUSNESS?

Before we get into the breastplate itself, let's dissect this word "righteousness". I know we've all heard that word tossed around a lot in church, but do you really know the meaning behind it? It's defined as "the quality of being morally right or justifiable, free from guilt or sin" (Credit: Merriam Webster's Dictionary).

PHYSICAL

The breastplate on a Roman soldier was worn right over their chest. It protected their lungs, heart, and other major organs from being damaged in battle. Just imagine them walking into battle with their chest exposed. It could leave them vulnerable for a deadly attack against their vital organs.

SPIRITUAL

Spiritually, the heart represents our mind and our emotions (Reference: https://bible.org/seriespage/23-belt-truth-and-breastplate-righteousness). So, when Paul speaks about putting on the breastplate of righteousness, he is telling us to protect our minds and emotions from the enemy (Proverbs 4:23: Above all else, guard your heart, for everything you do flows from it). Satan will always try to keep you stuck in your feelings so you'll start to make decisions fueled by your emotions, instead of faith and obedience to God. Putting on the breastplate ensures that we remain in control of our emotions, instead of the other way around.

The breastplate can also be referring to Jesus, because He lived a sinless life. Like I mentioned before, God looks at His Son's righteousness that is now in us and not our own when we accept salvation. We no longer have to *work* our way to God. Disobedience (sin) opens the door for the devil to get into your mind/heart. We obviously cannot avoid sin completely because we all have a sin nature. This is why Jesus' righteousness needs to be our breastplate. We are righteous through Jesus Christ! If we rely solely on our own righteousness, we would be destined to fail because we are not perfect. Does this make sense? "Putting on the armor of God requires a decision on our part. To put on the breastplate of righteousness, we must first have the belt of truth firmly in place. Without truth, our righteousness will be based upon our own attempts to impress God. This leads to legalism or self-condemnation (Romans 8:1). We choose, instead, to acknowledge that, apart from Him, we can do nothing (John 15:5). We see ourselves as 'in Christ' and that, regardless of our failures, His righteousness has been credited to our account."

"As we wear Christ's breastplate of righteousness, we begin to develop a purity of heart that translates into actions. Wearing this breastplate creates a lifestyle of putting into practice what we believe in our hearts. As our lives become conformed to the image of Christ (Romans 8:29), our choices become more righteous, and these godly choices also protect us from further temptation and deception (Proverbs 8:20; Psalm 23:3)" (Reference: https://www.gotquestions.org/breastplate-of-righteousness.html/ What is The Breastplate of Righteousness (Ephesians 6:14)?).

HOW DO YOU PUT IT ON?
- ✓ Obeying God. Obey His commands in His Word and what He is convicting you of. Listen to what your Father is telling you to do.

Praise and Worship

- ✓ Guard your heart and control your emotions. Don't let the enemy keep you trapped in your feelings!

- ✓ Knowing that you are righteous because of Jesus' righteousness that lives in you! Whenever the enemy comes at you with condemnation or criticism, reminding you that you aren't perfect, put on your breastplate and boldly tell him, "I may not be perfect, but the one who lives in me and the one who died for me is! Because of Him, I'm set free from sin and I don't have to listen to you!"

- ✓ Living a righteous life. Learning to try and live free from the sin. "But the breastplate is not just imputed righteousness; it is also practical righteousness. When we are living a righteous life, we are protected from Satan. However, when we fall into sin, we give Satan an open door to attack and defeat us. Again, Ephesians 4:26-27 indicates this, as it says, "'In your anger do not sin': Do not let the sun go down while you are still angry, and do not give the devil a foothold." ... Sin opens the door for the devil into our lives. No doubt there are many Christians who, as a result of unrepentance, have psychological problems which are demonic in origin. There are Christians being tormented in their minds, bodies, emotions, work, and relationships because they have been handed over by God to the enemy until they repent. Ephesians 2:2 says Satan works in those who are "disobedient"; however, a righteous life is a protection" (Reference:

https://bible.org/seriespage/23-belt-truth-and-breastplate-righteousness/ The Belt of Truth and the Breastplate of Righteousness).

We "put it on" by seeking God and His righteousness above everything else (Matthew 6:33). We make Him and His ways our dwelling place (Psalm 91:1). We delight in His commands and desire for His ways to become our ways (Psalm 37:4; 119:24, 111; Isaiah 61:10). When God reveals an area of change to us, we obey and allow Him to work in us. At the point where we say "no" to God, we open a little crack in the armor where Satan's arrows can get through (Ephesians 6:16)." (Reference: https://www.gotquestions.org/breastplate-of-righteousness.html/ What is The Breastplate of Righteousness (Ephesians 6:14)?).

SHOES OF PREPARATION OF THE GOSPEL OF PEACE (EPHESIANS 6:15)

WHY WOULD SHOES BE SYMBOLISM FOR THE GOSPEL? WHAT DOES IT MEAN, "THE PREPARATION OF THE GOSPEL"?

Praise and Worship

PHYSICAL
Their shoes "...were studded with nails or spikes, like cleats, to help him keep his balance in combat" (Reference: https://www.gotquestions.org/gospel-of-peace.html/ What is the Readiness of The Gospel of Peace (Ephesians 6:15)?).
Let's break this piece of armor down a little since it's got a pretty long title to it.

SPIRITUAL
WHAT IS THE GOSPEL?
Let's get a little refresher of what the Gospel is. It is the message that God loves us so much that He sent His only Son to die for us on the cross so that we didn't have to.

WHAT PEACE?
It is the peace that comes from the knowledge that, once you accept salvation, you will not be subjected to God's wrath and will spend eternity in His presence after death. It is a day-to-day peace (Jesus protecting and strengthening you in your daily walk

Praise and Worship

with Him) and an eternal, spiritual peace (eternal life with God after death). The peace that comes from the Gospel will give you the confidence you need to withstand the enemy's attacks. It acts as the nails or spikes, planting us firmly in the peace that God has given us. It is our foundation! It is what keeps us steady and standing as we walk through life.

PREPARATION FOR WHAT?
Why is the word "preparation" in the description? Because we must know that the enemy will try and attack us on a daily basis. With the Gospel of Peace as your foundation, regardless of any situation, you know that with God on your side, you're going to get out of it. This is "because the enemy always aims to separate believers from God. It is God who gives believers the strength to put on God's armor and the power to conquer the devil. Therefore, the enemy always seeks to separate Christians from the source of all that is good" (Reference: https://bible.org/seriespage/24-footwear-peace-and-shield-faith). No matter what the enemy tries to tell you, put them shoes on and stand your ground!

HOW DO YOU PUT IT ON?
- ✓ When I was learning about this particular piece of armor, I came across something really interesting. The shoes can be used defensively and offensively. On the defense, we use them as an anchor to help us stand tall against the attacks of the enemy. Offensively, they're used for us to spread the Good News. (In addition to standing our ground, shoes are also for moving. God expects us to go on

the offensive and take the gospel of peace to others. **First Peter 3:15** says, "Always be prepared to give an answer to everyone who asks you to give the reason for the hope that you have." Sharing our faith is one of the best ways to maintain our own sure footing. God knows that when we are active in speaking of Him to others, we not only charge into Satan's territory, but we dig our shoes more deeply into truth and will be much harder to dislodge. When we have "studied to show ourselves approved unto God" (**2 Timothy 2:15**), we are ready to stand firm in the gospel of peace no matter what the enemy brings against us (**2 Thessalonians 2:15**)" (Reference: https://www.gotquestions.org/gospel-of-peace.html/ What is the Readiness of The Gospel of Peace (Ephesians 6:15)?).

- ✓ Meditate on the Gospel! Hide it in your heart and ask God to help you accept it in its entirety. Make sure you understand the significance of it. Wake up every morning and know that you are a sinner saved by God's everlasting grace! It's knowing that God not only sent His Son as a sacrifice for everyone collectively, but for you individually! It's remembering that Christ died to act as the bridge between us and God.

Testimony: Once I knew that God really loves me and that He is the only who saved me from myself, I began to feel my confidence shift. I felt less and less anxiety and fearful. I began to feel like whatever I faced, God would get me out of it. We are in the enemy's territory and we have to have solid and unmovable footing when walking through the battlefield. (1 Chronicles 29:15: We are foreigners and strangers in your sight, as were all our ancestors. Our days on earth are like a shadow, without hope).

THE SHIELD OF FAITH (EPHESIANS 6:16)

WHY IS FAITH REPRESENTED BY A SHIELD?

PHYSICAL

We all know what a shield does. It serves as protection from the opposing army.

SPIRITUAL
WHAT IS FAITH?
Let's run through what it is to remind us really quick.
- Hebrews 11:1 says that faith is "the substance of things hoped for the evidence of things unseen." It's being hopeful for the future, even if you can't see any progress or forward action yet.
- It is needed for us to know that God exists and to obey Him.
- Faith keeps us going and obeying God even when we don't yet see signs of a possible outcome. When He commands us to do something, we have to believe that there is a reason He is telling us to do it, even when we may not know it. It pushes us into the promises that God has waiting for us...which pleases Him. It is showing your commitment to His call on your life!

WHY IS FAITH A SHIELD?
- It acts as our first line of defense against the attacks of the enemy. Paul says in the passage that the shield "quenches the fiery darts of the wicked one." If we don't walk in faith every single day, we're going to be defeated every time the enemy attacks us with fear, anxiety, and doubt. Paul also tells us to "TAKE UP our shield..." in Ephesians 6:16. Keywords being "take up". A shield won't work if it isn't held up by the soldier and placed in front of him! During

this fight, always go in with faith being at the forefront!
  - It protects the rest of the armor. "While the rest of our armor helps protect us from Satan's onslaught, it is not what you ideally want to be using to absorb every hit. You do not, for instance, go out into battle intentionally blocking everything with your head. When our faith in God's omnipotence and care is strong, it is impossible for Satan to break through our shield and land an attack. But when we allow doubt to creep in, as Peter did when distracted by the waves, we will start to sink. The rest of our armor will be battered, and so will we. But an actively raised shield of faith prevents this otherwise inhibiting fatigue" (Reference: http://www.freebiblestudyguides.org/bible-teachings/armor-of-god-shield-of-faith.htm/ Lesson 5: The Shield of Faith).

- We can use faith as a line of offense. It's a way we can fight back against the enemy. "When Christ was being tempted by Satan, His faith in the Word and commands of God repelled Satan for a time (Hebrews 4:15 tells us that Christ was tempted in all things, so this was certainly not the only encounter Christ had with the devil). The boss (the metal knob in the middle) on the Roman shields allowed soldiers to give their enemies a stun-inducing shove that would allow them to follow through with an attack. Our faith in God, as demonstrated by Christ, can also give Satan a good shove backwards and give us a chance to fight back by *doing* God's will and work. Because God tells us that faith cannot just be in our minds, it must produce actions—works of obedience and service (James 2:20)" (Reference: http://www.freebiblestudyguides.org/bible-teachings/armor-of-god-shield-of-faith.htm/ Lesson 5: The Shield of Faith).

HOW DO YOU PUT IT ON?
- ✓ As the devil is throwing his attacks at you (doubt, discouragement, condemnation...), tell him, "My God will protect me. I have an all-powerful God who is on my side. He won't let me be defeated by you! No weapon you form against me will prosper (Isaiah 54:11)!"

- ✓ Recite God's promises that He speaks of in His Word; that is, all the blessings He's given you and what He's protected you from thus far. Remember, all the times God has come through for you. Remember the times that He showed up just in time. Writing them down really helps a lot. You can always have something to go back to when you need to have that reminder of His faithfulness to you.

HELMET OF SALVATION (Ephesians 6:17)

<u>**WHY IS SALVATION REPRESENTED BY A HELMET?**</u>

Praise and Worship

PHYSICAL

On the battlefield, the helmet protected the brain and head from injury. "When a soldier suited up for battle, the helmet was the last piece of armor to go on. It was the final act of readiness in preparation for combat. A helmet was vital for survival, protecting the brain, the command station for the rest of the body. If the head was badly damaged, the rest of the armor would be of little use" (Reference: https://www.gotquestions.org/helmet-of-salvation.html/ What is The Helmet of Salvation/Ephesians 6:17?).

SPIRITUAL
WHAT IS SALVATION?

Salvation is what we receive from God when we accept Christ as our Savior. It's when we realize that we aren't able to save ourselves from His wrath and judgment against our sins. So, how do these two things make the helmet of salvation?

WHY IS SALVATION A HELMET?

I've seen the helmet work in three ways:

1. Look at it this way, the mind is a battleground and the devil is trying to win victory over it (the invisible fight). He knows that our thoughts have so much power, so he'll try to sneak his way into our minds by planting little "what if" thoughts and doubts to have us second-guessing our faith. "The helmet helps to protect our thoughts from the enemy and refocuses us on Jesus. Our enemy hates that we have chosen this path and will stop at nothing to destroy us because of it. Just as the helmet protects the vital but vulnerable head from otherwise fatal blows, the hope of salvation can protect our thoughts from our enemy's attacks and temptations to disobey God.

Praise and Worship

Matthew 13:22: Now he who received seed among the thorns is he who hears the word, and the cares of this world and the deceitfulness of riches choke the word, and he becomes unfruitful" (Reference: http://www.freebiblestudyguides.org/bible-teachings/armor-of-god-helmet-of-salvation.htm/ Lesson 6: Helmet of Salvation). Our minds are battlefields. The outcomes of those battles determine the course of our lives. **Romans 12:1–2**instructs us to renew our minds by allowing the truth of God's Word to wipe out anything contrary to it. Old ideas, opinions, and worldviews must be replaced. We must allow God's truth to continually wash away the world's filth, lies, and confusion from our minds and adopt God's perspective" (Reference: https://www.gotquestions.org/helmet-of-salvation.html/ What is The Helmet of Salvation/Ephesians 6:17?).
Satan loves to keep us stuck in habitual sin and stunt our growth in Christ. The helmet reminds us that, even if the enemy tries to keep us in our sin, because of our salvation, we have already overcome it. It no longer has control over us, and we are no longer slaves to sin. We don't belong to the enemy anymore; we are now part of Christ's Kingdom! "Because of the power of the cross, our enemy no longer has any hold on us (**Romans 6:10; 8:2; 1 Corinthians 1:18**)" (Reference: https://www.gotquestions.org/helmet-of-salvation.html/ What is The Helmet of Salvation/Ephesians 6:17?).

2. The helmet also acts as the assurance of knowing that, no matter what the enemy tries to throw at you while you're

living here on Earth, you are promised an eternal life with God after death, and that you have a reward waiting for you on the other side! You already have the victory over the devil! No weapon that is formed against you shall prosper! Live in that truth!

HOW DO YOU PUT IT ON?
- ✓ Wake up and renew your mind every day, throughout the day! Reassure yourself that you have been saved and already have the victory! Focus on God and place your hope in Him, knowing that you are going to come out of whatever situation you are in.

- ✓ Have an eternal perspective. It's remembering that you will one day see God and spend eternity with Him. You never have to worry about separation from Him! "Keep an eternal perspective. When life crashes in around us, we must remember to look up. Our salvation is the most precious gift we have received. Keeping our eyes on that can help us weather life's storms. We can choose to live our lives by the motto 'If it doesn't have eternal significance, it's not important' (see Matthew 6:20; 1 Corinthians 3:11–13)" (Reference: https://www.gotquestions.org/helmet-of-salvation.html/ What is The Helmet of Salvation?/Ephesians 6:17)

- ✓ Learn to recognize when a negative thought is trying to creep in and immediately shut it down. The longer you let it fester, the deeper it is going to lodge itself into your mind and eventually your heart. "After all, our thoughts lead to our feelings and our feelings lead to our actions. It all begins with a thought and the only way to change that is to renew our minds" (Savannah Parvu). "Christians have been called out of this world. Though we remain in it, we are not of it and remain separate from it. Our way of living and even *thinking* should differ from the world's. We are to develop the mind of Christ (see Philippians 2:5), and as we have seen, that means having God's laws written on our hearts and minds so we can remember to always obey God" (Reference: http://www.freebiblestudyguides.org/bible-teachings/armor-of-god-helmet-of-salvation.htm/ Lesson 6: Helmet of Salvation).

SWORD OF THE SPIRIT (EPHESIANS 6:18)
WHY IS THE SPIRIT A SWORD? WHAT SPIRIT COULD IT BE?

PHYSICAL

The Roman soldier needed to go through special training in order to learn how to use a sword properly. "Swords were used to protect oneself from harm or to attack the enemy to overcome or kill him. In both cases it was necessary for a soldier to get rigid training on the proper use of the sword to get maximum protection" (Reference: https://www.gotquestions.org/sword-of-the-Spirit.html/ What is the Sword of the Spirit?).

SPIRITUAL

It is God's Word also known as the Bible! It is compared to a sword again in Hebrews 4:12, which reads, "For the word of God is living and active, sharper than any two-edged sword, piercing to the division of soul and of spirit, of joints and of marrow, and discerning the thoughts and intentions of the heart." You know how soldiers had to train in order to use a sword? Guess what we have to do, folks? Our training involves getting familiar with the Word so we're able to discern what's of God and what isn't. Look at how Jesus interacted with Satan while fasting in the wilderness. Satan tempted Jesus three times, and each time, Jesus came back with a line of scripture to shut him up. Even when the enemy twisted scripture, Jesus knew God's Word well enough to know that what he was saying was not being used in the right context. That's deep. We have to dig into our Word and really study it for ourselves in order to know how to use it against our enemy.

HOW DO YOU PUT IT ON/USE IT?
Like the shield of faith, the sword of the spirit can be used defensively and offensively.

- DEFENSIVE: The way that we use it defensively against the enemy is pulling up scripture that will block whatever he is trying to throw at us. When he attacks you with doubt, throw a scripture of faith at him. When he's making you feel less than who you are, throw a scripture at him that says you're a child of the Most High God. Be bold and tell him all of the things that God has promised and who He says you are! Don't let him get to you! You have a whole book to tell him off with! Don't let him try and trip you up with half-truths and confuse you when you know in your heart exactly what God has told you. Push that devil back and shut his behind up with God's Word. That's why reading and remembering scripture is so important.

- OFFENSIVE: We use the Bible offensively by quoting scripture to speak life over our situations. What do I mean by "speak life"? It means to speak God-centered positivity, hopefulness, and faith to your situation. Our words have tremendous power. Proverbs 18:21 says it this way, "Death and life are in the power of the tongue: and they that love it shall eat the fruit thereof." So, when we see a negative situation or circumstance begin to surface in any area of our lives, what we must immediately do is speak God's Word over it. If we start to give in to that situation

Praise and Worship

and allow it to take control of our speech, it could have us stuck in a rut or pitying ourselves. It's all in our words, so choose them wisely because they make a difference!
- o We can also go on the offensive for someone else's situation when the Holy Spirit intercedes during prayer.

Now that we know the surefire way God has given us to combat the enemy and how to use it, are there any other things we need to know about getting through the transition? Are there any other methods of how to learn to advance in our walk with Christ? Let me share with you some of the things He's shown me. First, write down anything that stuck out to you about the armor of God. What caught your eye? Did the Holy Spirit really bring something alive to you on the page?

<u>WHAT HAVE I LEARNED ABOUT THE ARMOR OF GOD?</u>

_____

_____

_____

_____

_____

_____

OTHER HELPFUL HINTS FOR TRANSITION
I'm going to share with you a few other things that you should keep in mind to help with the transition.

DISCOVER THE THINGS THAT TRIGGER YOU TO GO BACK TO YOUR OLD LIFESTYLE

- This goes back into how you need to let go of the things that keep you stuck in your old ways. There will be systems that the enemy will put in place in your life to trip you up, and it's up to each one of us to discover what they are. When you do, start coming up with your own system that will deflect his. For example, when you feel those temptations creeping up, listen to a gospel song, read a scripture out loud, or do something to redirect your mind back on God. I know for me, every single month like clockwork, the enemy tries to tempt me to step outside of God's command for me to stay pure in mind and body; every month, he rises against my abstinence. I've learned to stay away from things like certain movies or social media outlets that I know would tempt me to even think about breaking my vow of abstinence.

Praise and Worship

WHAT ARE SOME OF THE THINGS THAT I MAY HAVE TO GET RID OF (if applicable)? WHAT ARE MY TRIGGERS?

_____
_____
_____
_____
_____
_____
_____
_____

READ SCRIPTURE OUT LOUD /SET ASIDE TIME EVERYDAY TO READ THE WORD

- I've said this before —your words make a huge difference in your life. Research some scriptures that pertain to your current struggles and say them out loud. I'm telling you, it makes you feel so empowered and at peace when you speak our Father's words over your situation! This helped me so much when I was trying to get my confidence back up. Just try it right now! Lookup a scripture that relates to something you're battling, go to a mirror, and read the scripture out loud to yourself! Watch what happens!

Praise and Worship

WHICH SCRIPTURE DID I PICK? WHAT HAPPENED AFTER I READ THE SCRIPTURE? WHAT DID I FEEL?

I CHALLENGE YOU TO READ ANOTHER SCRIPTURE TOMORROW MORNING! WRITE DOWN WHICH ONE YOU CHOSE AND HOW YOU FELT AFTERWARDS

Praise and Worship

_____
_____
_____
_____
_____

- **MAKE SURE YOU LEARN THE DIFFERENCE BETWEEN THE THREE VOICES IN YOUR HEAD—YOU, THE ENEMY, AND THE HOLY SPIRIT**
  I'm not going to lie, it's really hard to tell the difference between the three of these voices at times. But I'll say it again, don't be too hard on yourself during this time in your walk. If you're really trying to hear God's voice and you get it wrong, He knows your heart. He sees you trying your best to listen to Him (just don't use it as an excuse to make the same mistakes over and over again). Take a look at this meme that I saw on social media.
  https://fortifymylife.wordpress.com/2013/08/14/gods-voice-vs-satans-voice/
  It goes over how to tell the difference between God's voice and the enemy's voice. Just stay focused on reading His Word and praying to Him. That's how you recognize His voice. Normally, our voices are saying something that will give us the glory, or it may be something that we *want* to hear and not necessarily what we *need* to hear.

Knowing the difference between condemnation and conviction helps you to recognize the voices too. Here's a little reminder of what conviction is.

- "Conviction is the work of the Holy Spirit where a person is able to see himself as God sees him: guilty, defiled, and totally unable to save himself (John 16:8). Conviction functions differently for the Christian and non-Christian. For the non-Christian, conviction reveals sinfulness, guilt and brings fear of God's righteous judgment. Whereas, conviction in the believer brings an awareness of sin and results in repentance, confession and cleansing"(Reference: https://carm.org/dictionary-conviction).
- Condemnation: The enemy making you focus so much on a mistake you made that you forget that God has already forgiven you. He'll identify you by your sins and mistakes.

I also recommend the books *The Battlefield of the Mind* by Joyce Meyer and *Crash the Chatterbox* by Steven Furtick. Both of them have really helped me with knowing how to tell the difference between all the voices we may hear on a daily basis.

- **FIND A CHURCH HOME/SURROUND YOURSELF WITH LIKEMINDED PEOPLE**
  Find a Bible study group near you and find a church that preaches straight from the Word of God with no ulterior motives. Doing this, coupled with limiting your time with people from your past who encourage bad behavior will

Praise and Worship

allow you to find more people who are seeking a relationship with God like you. Find a church that has ministries who cater to where you are in life (singles' ministry, marriage ministry, youth ministry, etc.). It also helps to find a mentor or a mature Christian who can help and advise you in your walk with Christ.

DO I HAVE A BIBLE STUDY GROUP OR CHURCH TO ATTEND? DO I KNOW ANY CHRISTIANS MY AGE I COULD START TO HANG WITH?

_____

_____

_____

_____

_____

_____

_____

WHAT HAPPENS AS YOU ADVANCE IN YOUR TRANSITION?

As you start to let go of your past and begin to become the person God has called you to be, expect even more changes. Yeah, I know what you're thinking—more changes?!! Yes, more changes. You're maturing and growing in Christ so there will always be room for improvement. You have to continue to push yourself more and more as you grow in Him. He may reveal to you that there is a stronghold or behavioral pattern you never knew you had that is going to require a ton of work to get rid of. After a while, Bible study routines may not sustain you anymore.

Testimony: I started to notice that the systems I had in place for Bible study were becoming less and less effective. God revealed to me that, as I was maturing in Him, the ways I was studying couldn't stay the same if I wanted to continue forward. I had to study harder, focus more, and pray more. Whenever you feel like you aren't hearing God or not really learning anything from your Bible study, it is time to make a change! You have to pray a little longer than you used to and study a couple more verses a night. Take it as a good sign if you have to continually up your game. It means you're getting more and more mature! This means that you are going from milk to meat (Hebrews 5:12-14).

If you're in the beginning stages of your transition, DO NOT GIVE UP! Keep going. I know it's hard right now, but God will give you the strength you need to make it. I know there's a lot that you may have to give up and there may be some things you do not want to face from your past. But the suffering will end! Whatever is hard for you to fight now, is going to seem so easy to combat later. Whatever the enemy is throwing at you will pass.

Automatically, when we give our lives over to God, we are on the enemy's hit list. This Christian walk is a battleground, for

Praise and Worship

real. Let's look at who we're dealing with and why he has such a grudge against Christians. Write a couple more things down about your transition or soon-to-be transition.

What are my feelings (if applicable) about my transition now?

SATAN, OUR ENEMY

While I was writing, I remembered one of my favorite Tom and Jerry episodes where Tom had to be nice to Jerry in order to get into Heaven. In "Hell", Spike, the bulldog, was the devil; he was wearing a red suit, carried a pitchfork and laughed wickedly over a boiling pot.

(Image Reference: https://mugenarchive.com/wiki/Satan_(Tom_%26_Jerry)

If you haven't seen this episode, look it up, because it's a pretty good episode. Some people really do think of Satan as the

Satan, Our Enemy

dude in a red suit with a pitchfork. I've also heard it somewhere that people think Satan is someone we use to symbolize all of the evil in the world. Some may think he isn't real—that he's just some made-up character. But the Bible makes it crystal clear who this guy is and what his goal is. Folks, we really need to get to know our enemy and how he works. What is his problem and what does he want with us? But first, who do you think he is? What have you heard about him already?

WHO DO I THINK SATAN IS? DO I BELIEVE IN HELL?

IN THE BEGINNING….
If we're going to be real, I think we all picture Satan as a real ugly demonic-looking dude with horns, a tail and a set of hooves? Guess what? That's not him.

Who does the Bible say He is?
The scriptures say that he was the most beautiful angel and that he disguises himself as an angel of light (2 Corinthians 11:14: And no wonder, for Satan himself masquerades as an angel of light). Let's go back to the very beginning to see where he originated from.

Before creation and the fall of man, God created an angel that was far more beautiful than the rest; his name was Lucifer. Normally, we say that Lucifer was the music leader in Heaven. "It's often said that God placed Satan as the lead musician in Heaven, but no scripture says this for certain. Here are a few passages of scripture explaining and describing who God created him to be. "Was Satan the head musician? This cannot be answered definitively. Scripture does not say enough about what his duties were in heaven. Considering the fact that the angels constantly worship God (Isaiah 6:3; Revelation 4:8), it is possible that Satan led that worship. One thing is sure: for Satan to rebel despite having such an exalted position and close relationship with God, the devil is surely due to his eternal destiny (Revelation 20:10)" (Reference: https://www.gotquestions.org/Satan-music.html/ Was Satan in Charge of Music In Heaven?). "Satan was clearly a leading or the leading angel in heaven, but it is unclear whether he served as leader of the music"

(Reference: https://www.compellingtruth.org/Satan-music.html/ Prior to His Fall, Was Satan in Charge of Music in Heaven").

HIS FALL (Isaiah 14 and Ezekiel 28)

So, how, when, and why did Lucifer fall? " The angels were created before the Earth (Job 38:4-7). Satan fell before he tempted Adam and Eve in the Garden (Genesis 3:1-14). Satan's fall, therefore, must have occurred somewhere after the time the angels were created and before he tempted Adam and Eve in the Garden of Eden. Whether Satan's fall occurred hours, days, or years before he tempted Adam and Eve in the Garden, scripture does not specifically say" (Reference: https://www.gotquestions.org/Satan-fall.html/ How, Why, and When Did Satan Fall From Heaven?).

At one point, Lucifer became prideful in his beauty and position and wanted to be more powerful than God; he wanted to have His position and receive all of the glory and honor that belonged to God. He submitted to his own will, instead of God's will. When he took his focus off of serving the Lord and what He wanted him to do—when he choose to start fulfilling his will, that was his downfall. It began the moment he said, "I will." "Satan turned from hearing God's voice and began to seek his own will. To put another will over God's is to say that His will is not perfect. When Satan said, "I will", sin began. God calls Himself by name, saying, "I AM" (Exodus 3:14). He does not give this name to anyone else. The one who wants to be something in himself is therefore in conflict with God, and is expelled" (Reference:

https://activechristianity.org/what-does-the-bible-say-about-satan). Of course, God, being all-knowing, knew of Lucifer's rebellion and punished him for his sin (which was actually the very first sin). He cast him out of Heaven and he is now ruler of the Earth. He was created as Lucifer, but after his fall, his name became Satan. When he fell, he even persuaded one-third of God's angels to follow him. Guess what we call them now? Demons.

HIS GOAL/PURPOSE

John 10:10 makes it crystal clear what his goal is— "The thief comes only to steal and kill and destroy." There are several things that Satan wants to try and stop in the life of a believer (which I will address in a minute). How, why, and when did Satan fall from heaven? What is his main goal? "Satan wants to stop God's ultimate plan—salvation, new heaven, new earth and his demise" (Reference: https://www.allaboutgod.com/why-did-god-create-satan-faq.htm/ Why Did God Create Satan). After the fall of man, when God was handing out the punishments to Adam and Eve, He told Satan what his future will hold. (In Genesis 3:15, God prophesied that the serpent (Satan) would bruise the heel of the Seed of the woman, but Jesus—the Seed of the woman—would crush the serpent's head. The defeat of Satan in one sense has already occurred. The Crucifixion and Resurrection of Christ guaranteed Satan's doom" (Reference: https://answersingenesis.org/answers/biblical-authority-devotional/what-is-in-satans-future/ What Is in Satan's Future?/Biblical Authority Devotional: The Seventh C, Part 8). Throughout the Bible, we see where he tries to eliminate the

possibility of him being defeated by Eve's Seed. Take a look—
Satan's attempts at stopping God's plan:
- The killing of infant boys in Exodus (Exodus 1)
- Herod ordering the killing of infant boys (Matthew 2:16-18)
- Satan tempting Jesus in the wilderness (Matthew 4:1-11)
- Attempt to kill all Jews (Esther 3:12-14)

And what's his goal in the life of the believer? They are:
- To keep us from fulfilling our God-given purpose.
- To stop spreading God's love and Good News to the world.
- To steal our joy and faith in God.
- To persuade us to not to put God first.
    - Time spent alone with Him.
    - Not putting Him in charge of our lives/allowing Him to lead us in every aspect of our lives.

WHY HE ATTACKS US

Satan is permitted by God to mess with us but not gain victory over us (look at the story of Job). But the question is, why does he? What's his deal with us? I never really thought of it this way, but I remember reading somewhere that Satan is not only jealous of God, but he's jealous of us too! And there are a couple reasons why:

1. **We worship God and not him.** Okay, look at this—as Christians, we worship the Most High God, right? If Satan fell because he wanted to be God, wouldn't it make sense that he's jealous because we aren't worshipping him? He's not only jealous of our worship, but also of our

relationship and closeness with God. Angels do not have the same kind of interaction and relationship that we have with God. There are a whole lot of differences between angels and humans—which leads us to the next point.

2. **The effort God put into creating us.** We, as humans, were also created by God so much different than angels. Unlike them, we are able to marry, reproduce, and harbor amazing creativity "God has unique creative power, but Jesus says that in heaven, we will be like the angels, neither giving nor taken in marriage. Angels don't have children, they don't have the kind of creativity that we have. We human beings have been given an amazing gift by God. A man and a woman, in their coming together, can create something immortal. That's breathtaking. And the devil hates us for this" (Reference: https://relevantradio.com/2018/07/why-the-devil-is-jealous-of-you/). Lucifer was an angel, right? So, it makes sense that he's jealous of us since God put special work into creating us.

3. **We will be glorified after suffering for Christ's sake.** If Satan is already jealous of us, it's just adding insult to injury that we be glorified after he messes with us for following Jesus.

We know a few of the reasons why Satan attacks us (you can read up on more of them here: (Reference: http://www.pacificcog.org/transcript/120112RR.html/ The

Jealousy of Satan/ Rick Railston). How and when does he attack us? Let's start with the "when".

WHEN DOES HE ATTACK US??

Expect the enemy to attack you at any time as you grow and mature in Christ. He is looking for every and any opportunity to keep us bound to our pasts, unable to move forward so that he can sneak up on us when we're not paying attention. This is why the Word says to always be on guard. First Peter 5:8 reads,"Be on your guard. Your enemy the devil is like a roaring lion. He prowls around looking for someone to chew up and swallow." (Now, I'm not saying to be scared, looking over your shoulder at all times and constantly living in fear. Just be alert, is all I'm saying. Don't take it to the extreme.) Even though he can attack at any time, God has shown me that there are certain times in a Christian's life that we can expect the enemy to show up. And trust me, I've experienced an attack each one of these times in my life. Please note that anything that the enemy does to you has to get approved by God first! He has no authority or power to attack you without God allowing it to happen (look at the story of Job)! But here are the two common times that Satan attacks:

1. When he sees God begin to align things in your life for His glory and give you favor.
2. When we begin to put God first and go through sanctification.

Here's a list of examples of what I'm talking about:
- After salvation
- Before receiving a breakthrough or a blessing
- During healing/repentance

- As you begin to pursue your God-given purpose
    - Leading others to Christ
    - Praying/encouraging others
- When we're young

WHY DOES HE ATTACK US DURING THESE TIMES IN OUR LIVES?

Unlike us, the enemy sees what happens in the spirit realm. Humans, being temporal beings, can only see what's going on in the physical. "Whatever is happening in the spirit realm, manifests in the physical"—Joshua Eze. So, when Satan begins to see God rearranging things in the spirit realm, he knows something is about to happen, and he wants to try and stop it. He'll see you changing your ways of thinking, putting God first, becoming spiritually mature, and that's when he strikes! He sees your value and believes that you can spread God's love and advance His Kingdom. So, if it seems like every chance the enemy gets, he's attacking you from all directions, and you feel like you're not getting anywhere, doesn't mean that he is winning, my friend. He sees your progress; he sees God about to bless you. Look at the story in Daniel 10. Daniel prayed to God for 21 days for an answer to a vision he'd received. He prayed and fasted for 21 days with no answer. But little did Daniel know, his prayer had been answered, but Satan was battling the angel assigned to deliver the answer to Daniel's prayer! See? We really don't know what's going on behind closed doors (that's why faith is so important).

Now, let's get into detail on some of the ways the enemy attacks us. But first, jot some things down in these next two sections! Thanks for being a trooper and sticking around this long.

HAS THE ENEMY TRIED ATTACKING ME ALREADY?

HOW DO I THINK SATAN ATTACKS MANKIND?

TWO TYPES OF ATTACKS
I've noticed that the enemy's attacks fall into two categories—personal and global. Here's the difference between the two.
- PERSONAL: your own experiences. Things that no one else had to go through, struggles, insecurities, or negative encounters with others.
- GLOBAL any issue or topic that affects people on a national or global scale. Anything that affects a large group of people.

Let's go into detail about personal attacks first.

PERSONAL ATTACKS
IN OUR YOUTH
One thing we have to understand is that, even though he is not all-knowing like our Father, Satan is extremely wise. He's been around a heck of a lot longer than we have, and he knows a

lot more than we do. He knows the way humans work and think. He looks at our patterns and our family histories and can use it against us when given the opportunity. Oftentimes, the enemy loves to start coming for us at a very young age. He could be embedding deep wounds and hurts that will stay with us so long that we won't even realize they are there. As you grow up, he sees your potential to become a great representation of Jesus Christ and His Kingdom, and he wants to destroy any chance of you becoming who God has called you to be. I remember listening to one of Joshua Eze's lectures one day. He talked about how Satan often starts planting lies when we're young so that they won't get a chance to be pulled out when they need to be. Over time, those seeds will fester and grow into strongholds and walls around our hearts, all the way into adulthood. More importantly, the enemy wants to thwart our views of God, other people, and ourselves. And he loves to do it in our youths (bad experiences with church, how our parents/guardians raised us can also change how we see God). God willing, I will go deeper into this in another book.

Testimony: I know firsthand that God has had to heal me from past hurts that I have let linger in my spirit and mind for far too long. Those wounds soon turned into deep, DEEP strongholds that needed time to heal and repair. They became defense mechanisms when I got older.

HE ATTACKS IN OUR YOUTH THROUGH FAMILY PATTERNS

The enemy can look into our families' history and determine which type of demon or spirit has caused our lineage to stray from God, not accomplish our purpose or mess up our views of Him. Without anyone in the family realizing it, the same type of misfortunes and experiences can get passed down to each generation, with no one getting any healing or breaking the cycle. This is what's called a generational curse (even though a lot of these curses can begin in our youth; some of them may not manifest until adulthood). The curse itself can be a type of mindset, lifestyle, health issue, or experience. Each of them has a certain spirit or demon attached to it. Here's a list of the common types of generational curses:

- PHYSICAL
    - Rape, molestation
    - Abuse
    - Addiction
    - Barrenness
    - Sickness/disease

- EMOTIONAL/MENTAL
    - Bullying
    - Abuse/neglect
    - Mental illness
        - Narcissism
        - Spirit of Jezebel

- SPIRITUAL
    - Abuse
        - Using Bible to threaten/take out of context
        - Using religion to control or manipulate someone

- Use of witchcraft
- Involvement in the occult/secret societies

- **RELATIONAL**
    - Divorce
    - Unhealthy relationships
        - Putting a man before children
        - Codependency
        - Dominant woman, passive man (Spirit of Jezebel and Spirit of Ahab)
    - Abandonment

- **MONETARY/FINANCIAL PROBLEMS**
    - Spirit of poverty

HOW ATTACKS IN YOUR YOUTH AFFECT YOUR ADULT LIFE

I mentioned before that immediately after we accept salvation, the problems and issues we had beforehand do not go away. That includes any suppressed memories and emotions from our youth. Any traumatic childhood experiences MUST be acknowledged and dealt with as soon as possible, because this is where the enemy will attack you first.

WHY DOES THE ENEMY WANT TO KEEP YOU STUCK IN YOUR PAST?

If you continue to just let things fester, don't acknowledge your hurt and suppress emotions, it'll become harder and harder to break free from the pain. If you're not careful, past hurts can manifest into strongholds. "A stronghold is an area of darkness within our mind or personality that causes ongoing spiritual, emotional and\or behavioral problems. We can be genuinely born-again, and sincere in our faith, but have an ongoing struggle with thoughts, emotions, and habits that wage war against our relationship with Christ. We pray, we study, and we attempt to discipline ourselves, but often find our "problem" is resistant to real change" (Reference: https://christianarmor.net/spiritual-warfare/3-spiritual-strongholds/ Spiritual Strongholds).

COMMON STRONGHOLDS:
- Pride
- Anxiety/worry
- Bitterness/unforgiveness

There are some things we may not want to address from our pasts; this is because the memories hurt too much and it will take time, effort, and discipline to get through it all. Nevertheless, the quicker you come to grips with your past, the quicker the healing process can begin. "You are either redeemed from your childhood or still broken from it" (Loosely quoted from Joshua Eze).

Testimony: In my own life, low self-esteem and self-doubt were embedded in me somewhere around middle school. I let it fester and I let it take hold of me, to the point where I was unable to control my emotions and didn't know how to really express myself. Understanding what happened in your past will allow you to know where your weaknesses are and what you need to work on. Self-awareness is really important so you know where the enemy may try and attack you. You have to stop making excuses and using your past to justify you acting out negatively or harboring negative personality traits. The enemy wants you to use your past as an excuse to not fully trust God or heal from your brokenness; he wants to ensure that you remain spiritually immature. He will try to have you stuck in your ways, refusing to let the Lord heal you and mold you into the person He created you to be!

Satan knows how powerful a testimony can be. He knows that if you allow God to lead and heal you, your testimony will motivate and inspire other people to follow Him as well. So, what does he do? He's going to try his best to keep you from maturing. I've heard someone say the enemy wants to do one of two things with your testimony:

1. Keep you quiet by utilizing the spirit of fear to cause you to worry about what people may say or out of fear of judgment.

2. Dilute your testimony with pride so you only show the blessings God has given you, but not where He's brought you from (past hurts, mistakes, etc.)/no transparency. What this does is keeps people looking at God's hand (what He can give us) and not His heart.

Don't let your past hold you back from what God has in store for you, brother or sister. He wants to bless you, but He can't if you're holding on to the things that hurt you. Just let God help and heal you so that you're able to move forward. Shame the devil!

WHAT EVENTS FROM MY PAST ARE THE ENEMY TRYING TO KEEP RELEVANT?

___

***I want to encourage you to either seek counseling or speak to a mature Christian about your past. Holding that stuff in does nothing positive for you and will keep you bound. Give it to God and let it go! I know that it's easier said than done but putting it in God's hands will ensure that you'll get the healing you need! You can make it! James 5:16** says, "Confess therefore your sins one to another, and pray one for another, that ye may be healed. The supplication of a righteous man availeth much in its working."

Satan, Our Enemy

HOW HE ATTACKS US ON A DAY-TO-DAY BASIS
ATTACKING OUR MINDS

Do you remember when I mentioned that we are in a never-ending battle in our minds against the enemy, right? That invisible war? This is the battleground where we're going to be fighting Satan the most. But exactly how is he able to attack our minds? Can he read our minds? Does he have the ability to implant thoughts into our minds? To answer one of those questions, he is NOT able to read our minds. In the Bible, it says, "Even before a word is on my tongue, behold, O Lord, you know it altogether" (Psalm 139:4). It would take omniscience for Satan and his demons to read our minds, which they do not have" (Reference: https://www.gotquestions.org/Satan-read-minds.html/ Can Satan Read Our Minds or Know Our Thoughts?). I don't know about you, but sometimes, I would have thoughts come into my head and I would have no clue where they came from. Just nasty, negative, horrible stuff. Satan is not all-knowing, but he does have some knowledge of who we are. "However, Satan and his demons have been observing and tempting human beings for thousands of years. Surely, they have learned a few things about us over the years. Even without the ability to know our thoughts, they can make a well-educated guess as to what we are thinking and then attempt to use that to their advantage" (Reference: https://www.gotquestions.org/Satan-read-minds.html/ Can Satan Read Our Minds or Know Our Thoughts?).

As I was researching if Satan has the ability to plant thoughts into our heads, I didn't find anything in scripture that clearly says that he does. One article I read put it this way, however: "I can think of no passage which specifically states that Satan can do this by directly tampering with our minds, i.e., inserting thoughts apart from some instrument, but he certainly has a multitude of ways by which he seeks to influence our thought processes through the world system over which he rules as the one called the god (ruler) of this world or age (2 Corinthians 4:4; John 12:31). This seems to be the general focus of scripture on his many schemes, temptation, and deceptions." ..."We all wonder at times just where some of our thoughts come from and it may be that, if we are not as focused on the Lord and His truth as we should be, Satan through his demon hosts can somehow raise thoughts and questions in our minds. John 13:2 is a passage which may support this, though we aren't told just how the devil put it into Judas' heart to betray the Savior. This could simply refer to the culmination of the processes of external temptations that affected Judas' own thinking because of his failure to respond and truly believe in Christ. In John 13:27 we are told that Satan entered Judas, but this was after the statement of 13:2" (Reference: https://bible.org/question/can-satan-put-thoughts-our-minds-can-be-used-tempt-us-sin/ Can Satan Put Thoughts In Our Minds That Can Be Used To Tempt Us To Sin?).

At times, I do believe that somehow, he is able to whisper things into our ears that cause doubt or remind us of our pasts. How? Obviously, Satan uses words to attack us, right? And he can use those words in many different forms. They could be in the form of thoughts, half-truths (which was how he tricked Eve), suggestions, discouragement, words that were spoken by someone that you meditated on for too long. Satan knows the power that words have and it only takes one negative comment or one word of criticism to mess with your head. And if you think on them too long, his words can turn into strongholds or tempt us to go against God's will.

TEMPTATION

Why do I say this? Satan looks at what you're craving and longing for and plays on that. He'll dangle something in front of you that may look like it's better than what God has promised you. He always comes at you with what you think you want, need, or what you believe is good for you to get you to disobey God's commands. Take a look back at how Satan tempted Jesus in the wilderness. He saw that Jesus had been fasting for 40 days and 40 nights and knew that he was going to be hungry. Do you see that? He looked at what Jesus wanted and needed, and he used it in his first attempt to tempt Him. I have even heard someone say that before God sends the real thing, the enemy sends you a counterfeit (why it is always important to test every spirit. First John 4:1 tells us, "Dear friends, do not believe every spirit, but test the spirits to see whether they are from God, because many false prophets have gone out into the world").

HOW TO FIGHT TEMPTATION

- Be mindful about the things that you are craving and longing for. And make sure they do not turn into idols (literally, anything that you put before God in your life is an idol. Don't think that idols are just small statues that people worship). You must give the things that you crave and desire to God and let Him satisfy you.

- As hard as it can be at times, we have to be content with what God has blessed us with in whatever season we're in. Look to the Lord for your main source of joy, and be grateful for where He has you (1 Timothy 6:6-12: But godliness with contentment is great gain. For we brought nothing into the world, and we can take nothing out of it. But if we have food and clothing, we will be content with that. People who want to get rich fall into temptation and a trap and into many foolish and harmful desires that plunge men into ruin and destruction. For the love of money is a root of all kinds of evil. Some people, eager for money, have wandered from the faith and pierced themselves with many griefs. But you, man of God, flee from all this, and pursue righteousness, godliness, faith, love, endurance and gentleness. Fight the good fight of the faith. Take hold of the eternal life to which you were called when you made your good confession in the presence of many witnesses.) This definitely takes time and a lot of effort to do.
- Always find something to be thankful for and you won't be longing for anything as much. Keep a gratitude journal. Write something that you're thankful for every single day, no matter how small it is. It helps to remind you just how blessed you are so you won't worry about what you don't have.
- Test every spirit. Just because an opportunity presents itself for you to advance in life, doesn't mean it's for you. Not every opportunity is from God.
- HOW TO TEST A SPIRIT—Pray about it and ask yourself a

few questions—Does it contradict with what the Word says? Will it cause me to backslide to past sins? Will it give God all the glory?

- HOW TO KNOW IT'S NOT FROM GOD—Everything that Satan gives or promises comes with a price. You are always going to have to lose something in order to obtain it. The enemy plays on the idea that you think you know what you want, so he delivers it to you, and it is then that you realize that it came with a price. It comes dressed up as something you want but don't need. The enemy wants you to give something up in order to get something. Whether it be your family, time, energy, or maybe even your soul. If you find yourself continually sacrificing things and no fruit of the Spirit is producing in your life, it's from the enemy! He likes to convince us that we will be getting so much in return when we really won't get anything. Nevertheless, God's blessings are based upon His grace. We don't deserve them, nor can we earn them. He's not looking for anything in return; this is the true definition of unconditional love. God gives you what you NEED, which will end up being ten times better than what you *think* you want. Yes, we will have to work for some things, but in the process, you're growing, maturing and learning through Him.

We have all fallen into temptation in some way or another. We are not perfect. But with every setback and defeat, we become sharper, more mature and more keen to hear the voice of God and what direction He wants us to go in.

What ways has the enemy tempted me?
In what instances have I given into temptation?

FEAR

This one is self-explanatory, and it can come in many different forms. Fear of the future, fear of the unknown, fear of what people will think—If Satan can keep you stuck in fear, you won't be able to move forward in faith. He knows that fear will make you forget the presence of our Father. He will use the things that happened in your past against you, be it relational, professional, or anything. This also leads to the next point, since fear can be used globally as well.

No matter what the enemy may try and throw at you, keep telling yourself that greater is He who is in you! You're not a slave to sin, nor are you a slave to your old mindsets and strongholds anymore! You have already conquered them all through Jesus Christ!

Okay, so now we have an idea of how the enemy attacks us individually, but does he have any systems set up on a larger scale to attack us corporately? How do we know he's influencing things in society? Let's take a look...

ATTACKS ON GLOBAL SCALE

How do we know what the enemy's systems look like in the world? Remember that Satan fell because he wanted to be God. What he has done, in his attempt at being God, is created copies of the things that God has created. And everything that is a copy of God's original plan is a form of perversion. Perversion is "the alteration of something from its original course, meaning, or state to a distortion or corruption of what was first intended" (Reference: Google Dictionary). "Now, sadly, there are billions of wills that differ from God's among the human race and among the demonic legions that followed Satan's rebellion (cf. Revelation 12:2-4)." (Reference: https://www.compellingtruth.org/fall-of-Satan.html/ When Was The Fall of Satan, And How Did It Happen?) He puts systems in place to deceive us and to lead us away from God's original plan; his goal is to persecute Christians and fill our minds and hearts with his perversion. Satan's global systems of attack are viewed by the world as acceptable, even though they go against God's Word. Because the enemy's hand is on the world right now, nothing is in order. There is absolutely no kind of balance anymore. Everything is chaotic. Many people are following Satan's counterfeit lifestyle choices and indulging in his ideas, and it's showing in the current state of the world. The loss of the family structure, confusion of gender roles, the promotion of homosexuality, the continued rise of racism, and the promotion of selfishness are all parts of Satan's plan. I can go on and on. It's scary to see how far we have fallen. Why do you think there's so much hell in the world right now? And if you speak out against (even in a loving way) or don't agree with a certain idea or lifestyle, you're automatically considered a bigot, viewed as hateful, and are considered an enemy (Pro black, feminism, homosexuality—trust me, I'm not going to leave you in the dark about what God says about all of these issues). Everyone wants to blame God for all of the bad things going on right now, but look at how the world sees Him. We are trying to put our own will and what we think will make us happy over God's perfect will for us. Satan wants us to think that we don't need God, we can live to please only ourselves and we can be our own gods (Second Timothy 3:2: "People will be lovers of themselves, lovers of money, boastful, proud, abusive, disobedient to their parents, ungrateful, unholy").

Take a look at some examples (and I know that some of the things on this list are going to upset some people. Please be on the lookout for another book going into detail about each of these things):

- Fear
    - Through the use of media
        - Threat of wars
        - Bad politics
        - "Rise" of racism/police brutality
        - Possible outbreaks of disease
- False religions, New Age beliefs, Occult, witchcraft
- Legalization of abortion
- Gender confusion
    - Transgenderism/blending of the genders
    - Loss of gender roles
        - Increase of domineering women and weak men
        - Toxic masculinity/radical feminism
- Common destructive behavioral trends and mindsets
    - "false confidence"
        - Being "hard", "I don't need anyone", portraying confidence when actually

                insecure
        - Pride/full of one's self
        - Lack of empathy/not worrying about other's feelings/selfishness
- Lust/sexual perversion
    - Sensuality everywhere in media
    - Homosexuality/same sex marriage
- Idolatry
    - Love/sex/attention
    - Money
    - Self
    - Fame/acceptance/validation
- This scripture is a pretty good example of what we are seeing in the world right now—2 Timothy 3:1-2 warns us, "But mark this: There will be terrible times in the last days. People will be lovers of themselves, lovers of money, boastful, proud, abusive, disobedient to their parents, ungrateful, unholy."
- Saturation of the church/losing its potency in the world/becoming like the world
    - Prosperity preaching
    - Churches not preaching Gospel
    - Only about church attendance and money

WHAT IS SIN??

IS ONE SIN WORSE THAN THE OTHER?

The goal of Satan's attacks is to get us to go against God's Word and commands for our lives, or better yet, to get us to sin against Him. And let me get something out of the way really quick about sin. I used to believe that all sin was equal in God's eyes. I thought that He saw murder on the same level as lying, but this is not true. Although all sin, no matter what it is, results in the same consequence (eternal separation from God in Hell), there are different "degrees" of sin, if you will. Look at what I found as I researched this a little bit more: "In Matthew 5:21-28, Jesus equates committing adultery with having lust in your heart and committing murder with having hatred in your heart. However, this does not mean the sins are equal. What Jesus was trying to get across to the Pharisees is that sin is still sin, even if you only want to do the act, without actually carrying it out. The religious leaders of Jesus' day taught that it was okay to think about anything you wanted to, as long as you did not act on those desires. Jesus is forcing them to realize that God judges a person's thoughts as well as his actions. Jesus proclaimed that our actions are the result of what is in our hearts (Matthew 12:34). So, although Jesus said that lust and adultery are both sins; this does not mean they are equal. It is much worse to actually murder a person than it is to simply hate a person, even though they are both sins in God's sight. There are degrees to sin. Some sins are worse than others. At the same time, in regard to both eternal consequences and salvation, all sins are the same. Every sin will lead to eternal condemnation (Romans 6:23). All sin, no matter how "small" is against an infinite and eternal God, and is therefore worthy of an infinite and eternal penalty. Furthermore, there is no sin too "big" that God cannot forgive it. Jesus died to pay the penalty for sin (1 John 2:2). Jesus died for all of our sins (2 Corinthians 5:21). Are all sins equal to God? Yes and no. In severity? No. In penalty? Yes. In forgivability? Yes." (Reference: https://www.gotquestions.org/sins-equal.html/ Are All Sins Equal To God?). "First, not everybody is hurt in the same way by every sin. In other words, if I shoot Michael dead right now, or if I just spit on him, both are very ugly sins and Jesus calls hatred murder. But he's not dead if I only spit on him! So worse sin—meaning worse in its effect—would be killing over spitting. And I think we should say that. It is! Because consequences matter—at least for you! —and for me, I think, because here is another text we have to bring in. Jesus taught that there would be degrees of punishment. If you know the right and don't do it, you'll be beaten with more stripes than if you don't know the right and do wrong. So there's degrees of punishment, which must mean degrees of guiltiness, which must mean that some sins are more blameworthy than others" (Reference: https://www.desiringgod.org/interviews/are-all-sins-equal-before-god/ Are All Sins Equal Before God?).

Now, let's go a little more in-depth about what happens if you fall for any of the enemy's traps.

WHAT HAPPENS AFTER WE SIN?
As humans, we are going to mess up in one way or another every single day. So, what happens after we give in to the enemy's temptation or fall for his lies and sin? Between a Christian and someone who hasn't accepted Christ, it differs. Let's start with what happens when a Christian sins.

Satan, Our Enemy

CHRISTIAN "JUDGMENT"

God has and will forgive all of our sins when we accept Christ as our Savior. We will never have to worry about eternal separation from God (this is not an excuse to habitually sin)! But just like any other human, Christians will commit some type of sin every day. Once we put Him first in our lives, we will want to try our best to obey His commands (not sin). And when we do sin, a true Christian will immediately be led to repentance by the Holy Spirit (when I say "true" Christian, I am referring to individuals who have made the decision to accept Christ's salvation and allows Him to lead them in every part of their lives). We won't want to commit the same sin again. Now, what I don't want you to think is that, as a Christian, when you sin, your salvation goes away or that you'll have to get saved again. Jesus died for our past, present, and future sins, and your salvation does not go away. You cannot make it go away and Satan doesn't have the power to make it go away. Now even though, Christians don't have to worry about eternal separation, there may be consequences and negative experiences we have to face now (not in eternity) as a result of our sinning against God. Here's what Christians can experience after they sin:

- Condemnation. The enemy loves to lure you into sinning and then whisper lies to you afterward, for example, "Look at what you did. You ain't nothing but a no-good sinner. God will never use you now." He makes you feel like crap for the very thing he tempted you to do in the first place.
- Consequences of the act of sin. It may result In pain of some kind or losing something. Oftentimes, I've noticed that, even if there isn't an instant consequence from me

sinning, the guilt that I feel afterwards for letting my Dad down is enough for me to repent and not want to do it again.

- There are different kinds of consequences that can be physical, mental, and spiritual
  - Having to repeat the same lessons over again/delayed blessings.
  - "Feeling" distant from God. Even though God is with us wherever we go, sin can make us feel distant or disconnected from Him. I've experienced feeling distant from God spiritually, and I've felt like I had to work my way back into an intimate place with Him. It's a horrible feeling and I cannot stand it.

I definitely recommend reading "Have You Considered the Consequences of Sin?" by Jackson Wayne on ChristianCourier.com. He goes into further detail on the different consequences of sin.

Every night, say a prayer acknowledging any sins that you have committed that day and allow Him to reveal your unintentional or forgotten sins. This gives God the chance to correct you and for you to mature spiritually. You can't move forward when you don't address the issue, right?

UNBELIEVER'S JUDGMENT

I may step on a few toes right now with this next part, but

if I didn't share the whole truth with you, there wouldn't be any point to this book. Nowadays, a lot of people are preaching, believing, and only wanting to hear that God is all-loving, He accepts us as we are, and will always forgive us. Ladies and gentlemen, if you think that the God who is all-powerful, all-loving, and all-knowledgeable doesn't have something to say or doesn't have consequences for us when we against His Word, you are sadly mistaken. God didn't just create all of us and then have no rules for us to follow. If He didn't create boundaries for us, there would be absolute chaos (and since a lot of us aren't listening or obeying Him, look at how the world is now). He has an order for how nature and the world works, and He has an order for how we should be living as well. I mean, just look at it from His point of view. The God who created the universe is looking down on His creation, destroying one another and the world that He has given them to live in with no remorse. The world is disobeying His commands and believing that they themselves are their own gods. Imagine how He feels after sacrificing His only Son in order to have an intimate relationship with us and even giving us a step-by-step guide on how we should live. He gives us plenty of time and opportunities to repent and accept salvation, but we continually reject it and think that we can save ourselves. We refuse to believe that there will be consequences for not listening to the all-knowing God. Listen to me clearly, if you continue to reject what God has offered you, He will allow you to continue living the way you want, and when you pass away, you will be eternally separated from God in Hell. If you choose to follow the enemy, you're going to meet the same end that he will—forever separated from God and partaking of an eternal death.

And a little side note: **You cannot choose to be neutral.** There is no in-between. You're either a child of God and an enemy of the enemy or you're a child of the devil and an enemy of God. You will always be serving God or the enemy. Matthew 6:24 says it this way, "No man can **serve two masters**: for either he. will hate the one, and love the other; or else, he will hold to the one, and despise the other, Ye cannot **serve** God and mammon." If you aren't obeying God's Word and have not accepted Jesus as your Savior, you're serving the enemy. There is no such thing as living for yourself. This is a lie that is spreading like wildfire right now, and it is scary.

FINAL JUDGMENT

In the Bible, the book of Revelation speaks about the Tribulation or something called, "the End Times" (the church or all Christians will be "raptured" or ascend into Heaven before the Tribulation. Look at 1 Thessalonians 4:16-18). And if you look at different verses in the Bible about the end times (Matthew 24:1-51, 2 Timothy 3:1-5), we are definitely living in the end times. If you've ever heard of the movie "Left Behind", that's exactly what I'm referring to. During this period, God will lay His judgment down on the Earth in various, horrific ways (Revelation 6-18). Trust me, you don't want to be around during the Tribulation.

HOW TO BLOCK THE ENEMY'S ATTACKS AND AVOID FINAL JUDGMENT

Now that we know the when, why, and how of the enemy's attacks, let's get a refresher of some of the ways to block his attacks and how to avoid God's final judgment on humanity.

Satan, Our Enemy

WHAT METHODS OF BLOCKING HIS ATTACKS DO YOU REMEMBER? GO BACK A COUPLE PAGES IF YOU NEED TO 😊. HOW CAN YOU AVOID FINAL JUDGMENT?

_____

_____

_____

_____

_____

_____

_____

_____

- ✔ **FIRST AND FOREMOST, ACCEPT JESUS CHRIST AS YOUR PERSONAL SAVIOR!** I'm telling you this because I truly care about where you will spend eternity. I cannot stress this enough. We don't have to walk through life with shame, guilt, anger or resentment! Don't you want that? Don't you want to be free of what happened in your past? From what they did to you? The mistakes you made? God offers that solution through His Son!! You can be free and healed! He will do things for you far beyond what you could ever think or even ask! My God takes good care of His kids. Trust me. I am living proof! It's time to humble ourselves and accept the fact that we cannot make it on our own in this world, nor can we save ourselves from God's judgment against our sin. He sent His only Son to die for us so that we didn't have to. He made it so much easier for us to have an intimate relationship with Him. It's really not hard! Just accept Christ as your Savior and watch Him work wonders in your life!

- ✔ **USE YOUR ARMOR!** Remember to use the helmet of salvation to defeat the enemy's words! He's going to try everything he can to fill your head with confusion, but if you put on that armor every morning and focus on the One who made you, his lies and deceptions are just going to bounce right off of you. You're winning, even when it doesn't seem like it!

- ✔ **MANAGE YOUR FAITH!** No matter the type of attack, keep your faith strong. Trust and believe that no matter what you're up against, somehow, it is going to work out for your good! Romans 8:28 says, "And we know that all things work together for good to those who love God, to those who are the called according to His purpose." The enemy wants you to believe that God won't deliver you out of your situation and that there is no hope. Keep that shield up and your faith in the Almighty God, and He will

Satan, Our Enemy

fight your battles!

- ✓ **MAINTAIN A STRONG PRAYER LIFE!** As Christians, we need to be doing all of our fighting on our knees! Bad day, pray. Good day, pray. No matter what is happening, keep praying! Ask people to pray for you. PRAYER WORKS!

- ✓ **ALWAYS REMEMBER WHO YOU ARE** It's a sad, sad thing when the enemy knows who you are but you don't. Really come to terms with who God created you to be and build your confidence around that! Take a look at how God sees you. He says we're His children; we're fearfully and wonderfully made. He took the time out of His busy schedule to specifically make you! Embrace that!

- ✓ **REMEMBER WHO IS ON YOUR SIDE!** There's a scripture that my pastor says all the time. It is 2 Corinthians 4: 8-9, and it reads, "We are troubled on every side, yet not distressed; we are perplexed, but not in despair; persecuted, but not forsaken; cast down, but not destroyed." Even if it seems like the enemy is winning, God is always working behind the scenes! Just trust Him. First John 4:4—reminds us, "Greater is He that is in you, than he that is in the world." Do you know what that means? When you become a Christian, the Holy Spirit comes to live in you, right? And Satan is the ruler of this world. So, the One who lives in you is greater than the one who rules this world. God will never leave you or forsake you! He's got your back!

Your enemy will try everything in his power to get you to turn away from God and what He has planned for you, even if that means messing up your view of the church, perverting your opinion of God, or causing you to get hurt by people close to you. No matter what it takes to bind and control you, he's willing to do it. But know this—everything he does, in one way or another, will work out for your good, as crazy as it sounds. This is, of course, when you allow God to be first in your life. I know, I know. It's crazy to believe that the things that have happened to you will somehow be to your benefit someday, but look at me. If I didn't go through all that I went through, you wouldn't be reading this book right now. You wouldn't have learned all that you have from this book if I didn't go through all of the hell that Satan put into my life. And believe it or not, I'm just getting warmed up! I have so much more that I want to share with you. This is only the first of many books to come. He has healed me from so many things, shown me where I went wrong in the past, and I have never been at more peace in my life. I have tried a number of things in the pursuit of peace and happiness. Aren't YOU tired of looking for that missing piece in your life? Aren't you ready to start getting good sleep at night? This could be you. If you let God into your life, you'll experience the joy, peace, and happiness you never thought you could possess.

THE MILLION DOLLAR QUESTION—WHY IS CHRISTIANITY THE "TRUE OR RIGHT RELIGION"?

After all the things I've told you, why would anyone believe that all other religions in the world are false? Why should you believe that Christ is the ONLY way to joy, happiness, and

Heaven? I plan on answering this question in depth in my next book, but let me give you some solid points that really led me to switching from New Age beliefs to Christ. "However, sound reasoning tells us that all religions are not essentially the same merely because they contain some similarities. A brief survey of a few religions quickly reveals that each has competing, mutually exclusive claims. How, for example, can someone logically square the Hindu teaching that the universe is God with the Muslim belief that Allah, the God of Islam, is distinct from the universe? Thus, religions harbor irreconcilable differences, demonstrating that they cannot all possibly lead to the same God. Logically speaking, they can all be wrong, but they cannot all be right" (Reference: https://www.oneplace.com/ministries/bible-answer-man/read/articles/is-christianity-the-one-true-religion-8527.html/ Is Christianity The One True Religion?/ Hank Hanegraaff). In a world where you have access to whatever you want, however you want it, it makes sense that people want to pick and choose which religion best "suits" them. "But just like all roads don't lead to Indiana, all religions don't lead to Heaven" (Reference: https://www.gotquestions.org/right-religion.html/ What Is The Right Religion For Me?).

- **Historical evidence of Jesus' existence and resurrection**
    - Backed up by Atheist scholars
    - Over 500 witnesses of Jesus after the resurrection
    - Would have been difficult for disciples to have moved the body if Roman guards were in front of the tomb
- **Why would Jesus' disciples go to the grave and be tortured for someone who never existed or wasn't truly**

the Son of God?
- **No other religion has a deity like Jesus Christ**
    - Said to be the Son of God/ONLY way to Heaven
        - "Jesus said that He was the only way. Jesus is unique. He was either telling the truth, He was crazy, or He was a liar. But since everyone agrees that Jesus was a good man, how then could He be both good and crazy or good and a liar?" (Reference: https://carm.org/christianity-one-true-religion/ Is Christianity the One True Religion?/ Matt Slick).
    - Raised Himself from the dead
    - Eternal/part of the Godhead
    - The living Word of God
    - Fulfilled detailed prophecies
- **In order to get to Heaven and have a relationship with God, you must rely on faith in Jesus; this is not based on us working towards salvation (faith-based religion, not works based).**
- **Not just a religion, but a relationship.**
    - There are commands laid out for us in the Bible, but each relationship will differ based on the individual.
    - Only religion where God WANTS a relationship with His people, instead of Him being an unrelatable being we will never be able to communicate with intimately "...while every other religion would have humanity try to reach up to God, Christianity says

God reaches down to humanity. In other words, God's favor was obtained for humankind by Christ's life, death, and resurrection, and not by our own human merit". (Reference: https://www.oneplace.com/ministries/bible-answer-man/read/articles/is-christianity-the-one-true-religion-8527.html/ Is Christianity The One True Religion?/ Hank Hanegraaff)

- **The vast difference in how Christianity is viewed/portrayed in the world now compared to other religions and beliefs has led me to believe that there must be something truly unique about it.**
    - Oftentimes in movies and television, Christians are portrayed negatively.
        - crazy, judgmental, hypocrites
    - Jesus is mocked, but no other religious figure is mocked at all or to the magnitude that Jesus is.
    - People of other religions are praised for their public display of their beliefs, wearing their religious garments on a large, public platform.
    - Christianity is "attacked", mocked, or questioned oftentimes a lot more than other religions.

<u>GO BACK TO THE FIRST FEW PAGES OF THE BOOK AND SEE WHAT YOU JOT DOWN FOR WHAT YOU THOUGHT ABOUT CHRISTIANITY. ADD SOME MORE HERE IF YOU NEED TO.</u>

I know how you may view Christianity right now. You look at the people who claim to be Christian and many of them act like they don't have any kind of religion in them at all. The same people who say they follow Jesus will gossip about you or someone else behind their backs. Why would God let so much evil occur in the world? I get it! I understand you may have been hurt by church people in your past. Trust me, I've been there. Want me to prove it? Here's a list of what I thought Christianity was:

- I didn't want any part of it because God seemed like He just wanted to control you.
- I thought Christianity was like any other religion/all religions said the same thing.
- I saw people in the church acting just like people who didn't go to church. They even acted like they were better than everyone else.

- I've been deeply hurt by Christians throughout my childhood.

But, I am telling you this right now—please do not base your view of God on people! We live in a fallen world where people have been hurt, abused, and persuaded by the enemy. That doesn't mean that God is like those people; it doesn't mean that they actually follow Jesus. Don't continue to look at those people as an example of who God is! However, they act or however they have treated you, trust and believe they will have to answer to God about it.

ARE CHRISTIANS SUPPOSED TO JUDGE, TRY AND CONTROL OR FORCE PEOPLE TO CHANGE?

As Christians, our job is not to force people into believing in Christ, contrary to popular belief. We are not called to use His Word as a weapon of control or manipulation. Our assignment is:

- To introduce nonbelievers to a way of life that they never knew existed.
- To help them to know that there will only be one of two places we're going to spend eternity.
- To teach them that we aren't able to save ourselves, no matter how much we think we can.
- To plant the seed of salvation, teaching others how to allow Jesus Christ to become their Savior.

And that's exactly what I'm doing here. My goal is to encourage you to accept Jesus into your life and let Him save you. Just a quick PSA (Public Service Announcement) to all my fellow saints: we have to start getting serious about spreading the Gospel. We need to warn folks about where they are going if they have not accepted salvation. They have no clue what they are in for, and it is a real shame. I don't want another person to lose the opportunity to know Christ because I've kept my mouth shut. It's scary how many people don't know and choose not to listen to the truth because Satan has filled their heads with so much nonsense that they can't differentiate the truth from a lie. Satan has got people believing they can change God's order in how He created things! It ain't cool and it ain't the truth. We, as Christians, have to be getting brutally honest and stop trying to avoid any "taboo" topics when it comes to spreading the Word. The enemy is working double time, and we don't have time to be filtering our testimonies, prettying them up, or scared of offending people with the truth. We have to tell them, for example, "I know where you are. I've been there." We must show empathy!

WHAT DOES GOD ASK FOR UNBELIEVERS TO DO?

God loves you and wants a relationship with you! What He is asking you to do is accept that you are imperfect (sinner), that you are not able to make it in this life and after death without Him, and to receive His gift of salvation. God sent His Son to pay the price of sin for you and show the ultimate act of love. Jesus conquered death, hell and the grave so that we can have an intimate relationship with Him. He didn't want you to be eternally separated from Him! I cannot stress enough how God is trying to get your attention right now! He wants to change how you see Him and His people. There are so many people who choose to ignore God's gift of salvation simply because they don't have all the facts or their views of God are messed up. Our God is not an impersonal force who doesn't care for us and doesn't want or cannot speak to us. He wants a personal relationship with you and me! He doesn't ask you to wait until you "get yourself together" to come to Him, either. He will meet you right where you are! You don't have to do anything special to get His attention. No tricks, special chants or rituals. Open your heart up to Him and receive the love that He has for you! You don't ever have to wonder if God loves you again! There is no one else who can show you that kind of love like He has for you. No human being, career, degree—nothing in this world can satisfy you like our God can! If after reading this book, you want to accept Christ as your Savior from sin and eternal death, take a minute to say a prayer, inviting God into your life. I put a few down below, or you can just customize your own. Do whatever is on your heart. Say it genuinely, with true conviction, knowing that you are unable to make it without Him. He's waiting to hear from you. Say it out loud, write it down and post it on your wall—whatever and however you want to do it. It doesn't have to be this big, overexaggerated event. But doing this will open so many doors of healing, joy, and ultimately, eternal life for you! And a little side note, even if you don't feel some sort of crazy spiritual experience after saying the prayer, it doesn't mean it "didn't work". As long as you say your prayer with humility and honesty, you've accepted salvation!

"Father, I know that I have broken your laws and my sins have separated me from you. I am truly sorry, and now, I want to turn away from my past sinful life and return to you. Please forgive

me and help me avoid sinning again. I believe that your Son, Jesus Christ, died for my sins, was resurrected from the dead, is alive, and hears my prayer. I invite Jesus to become the Lord of my life and to rule and reign in my heart from this day forward. Please send your Holy Spirit to help me obey You, and to do Your will for the rest of my life. In Jesus' name I pray, Amen."
(Reference: https://www.allaboutgod.com/prayer-of-salvation.htm/ Prayer of Salvation).

"Jesus, I believe you are the Son of God, that you died on the cross to rescue me from sin and death and to restore me to the Father. I choose now to turn from my sins, my self-centeredness, and every part of my life that does not please you. I choose you. I give myself to you. I receive your forgiveness and ask you to take your rightful place in my life as my Savior and Lord. Come reign in my heart, fill me with your love and your life, and help me to become a person who is truly loving—a person like you. Restore me, Jesus. Live in me. Love through me. Thank you, God. In Jesus' name I pray. Amen" (Reference: https://www.ransomedheart.com/prayer/prayer-receive-jesus-christ-savior/ Prayer to Receive Jesus Christ As Savior).

YOUR SALVATION PRAYER
SO, WHAT IS CHRISTIANITY ABOUT AGAIN??

If you don't learn anything else from this book, please know this—Christianity is not about having to follow a bunch of rules, not having fun, and judging or criticizing other people. It's about accepting Jesus Christ as your Savior from sin and maintaining an intimate relationship with Him. It's about Him healing you and allowing you to spend eternity with Him after physical death! I wrote this book to tell you that it is possible to do a complete turnaround and put your Father first in your life. Regardless of what you thought was the truth, what you've done, and what has been done to you, our Father can fix it. I don't want you or anyone to think that Christianity is a religion that is impossible to live out. It is the only way to freedom and peace of mind. Take it from someone who has tried different ways of obtaining joy from other things. I want you to be encouraged to pursue a relationship with God. He is waiting for you! Right now! He is just waiting for you to finish reading the last page, and as soon as you close this book, He's looking for you to open your heart to Him. He's calling to you. Why do you think He led you to this book? Don't give Satan one more minute of your time and energy by feeding into his lies. Shame him by turning your life over to God.

BUT WHAT IF I STILL HAVE QUESTIONS?

For me personally, after experiencing life living with New Age beliefs, believing that all religions led to the same god, it was actually seeing Jesus move things around in my life that led me back to Him and back to my roots; this is what made me realize that He is real. Seeing how He pursued me and called me back to Him in my darkest hour and was the only one who was there for me. I was no longer just hearing about Him or only knowing Him based off of other people's beliefs. It was feeling His presence, watching Him answer my prayers that really solidified me believing that He's real. But I know that when defending your faith, simply using experiences without solid facts that support those experiences is not enough. I haven't gone into depth on a lot of the topics that stop people from becoming Christian or a lot of the controversial topics surrounding Christianity, such as:

- How do we know Christianity is the true religion?
- How do we know the Bible is true?
- Why is abortion wrong?
- Why is homosexuality a sin?

I had these same questions when I first gave my life to Christ, but there are legitimate answers that actually make sense to all of these questions! While waiting for my next book (that will answer all of these questions 😊), ask God, with a humble heart, to reveal some of these answers to you. When you go to Him for the answers, He will give them to you. You just have to be open-minded to the fact that, maybe, what you thought was the truth is actually a lie. I have had to uproot everything that I learned from my childhood, difficult and hurtful experiences, and from New Age beliefs. But it is possible! With God, all things are possible! The enemy wants us to fall just like he did. Each person who stays in bondage to sin and believes that they don't need Jesus is just another win for him. And I don't plan on letting him get anymore than he already has. I pray that by sharing what God has revealed to me about the current state of our world in relation to His Word and prophecy, I can win as many souls as I can for the Kingdom of God!

I'm so happy that you've made it to the end of my first book. Wow, this is amazing, not only to think that you've actually read my book until the end, but I was able to finish writing it.

There have been so many times when I wanted to just give up or I have put this book on the back burner, but it always seemed to creep back into my mind. I really pray that this has helped shed some light on the basics of Christianity and cleared up anything you may not have known about God. Again, be on the lookout for my next book that will really go into those hard questions that are relevant in today's world right now. I pray nothing but blessings and healing over your life. But before you close the book, take a look at the last couple pages for a complete list of places, names, holy days, and different words that we always hear thrown around in Christianity, along with their meanings and importance. It's like I said in the beginning of the book, I don't want you finishing this book without understanding the basics of Christianity.

I pray this has helped you in some way, and I cannot wait to share more stories of what God has revealed to me and what He has brought me through. I love you and Jesus loves you!

WEBSITES AND YOUTUBERS THAT HAVE HELPED ME UNDERSTAND CHRISTIANITY

WEBSITES
- Gotquestions.org
- Reasonsforjesus.com
- Desiringgod.com
- Bethinking.org

YOUTUBERS
→ Steve Bancarz
→ Doreen Virtue
→ Joshua Eze
→ Heather Lindsey
→ Tiffany Buckner (Anointed Fire)
→ Allen Parr (The BEAT)
→ Applygodsword.com
→ Whaddo you Meme?
→ Cross Examined

LISTS

COMMON CHRISTIAN/BIBLICAL WORDS

- SIN: anything that goes against God's commands.

- TRANSGRESSIONS: "a presumptuous sin, to intentionally disobey. When we knowingly run a stop sign, tell a lie, or blatantly disregard an authority, we are transgressing" (Reference: https://www.gotquestions.org/iniquity-sin-transgression.html/ What is The Difference Between Iniquity, Sin, and Transgression?).

- INIQUITIES: a premeditated choice to continue to sin without repentance that leads a person to no longer fear God (Reference: https://www.gotquestions.org/iniquity-sin-transgression.html/ What is The Difference Between Iniquity, Sin, and Transgression?).

- YOKE: not to be confused with "yolk", it is "Fitted on the neck of oxen for the purpose of binding to them the traces by which they might draw the plough, etc. (Numbers 19:2 ; Deuteronomy 21:3). It was a curved piece of wood called *'ol*.

- In Jeremiah 27:2 ; 28:10,12 the word in the Authorized Version rendered "yoke" is *motah* , which properly means a "staff," or as in the Revised Version, 'bar.'

"These words in the Hebrew are both used figuratively of severe bondage, or affliction, or subjection (Leviticus 26:13 ; 1 Kings 12:4; Isaiah 47:6 ; Lamentations 1:14 ; 3:27). In the New Testament the word 'yoke' is also used to denote servitude (Matthew 11:29 Matthew 11:30 ; Acts 15:10 ; Galatians 5:1)." (Reference: https://www.biblestudytools.com/dictionary/yoke/). It was used as symbolism to describe when a non-believer came together with a believer ("unequally yoked" 2 Corinthians 6:14).

- **LOVINGKINDESS:** "*Checed* (Hebrew) or lovingkindness, as it relates to the character of God, is most often used to describe God's heart toward those who are His own. Lovingkindness is God's kindness and steadfast love for His children, especially evident in His condescending to meet our needs" (Reference: https://www.gotquestions.org/lovingkindness.html/ What is Lovingkindness in The Bible?).

- **RIGHTEOUS/RIGHTEOUSNESS:** Dictionaries define *righteousness* as "behavior that is morally justifiable or right." Such behavior is characterized by accepted standards of morality, justice, virtue, or uprightness. The Bible's standard of human righteousness is God's own perfection in every attribute, every attitude, every behavior, and every word… On the <u>cross</u>, Jesus exchanged our sin for His perfect righteousness so that we can one day stand before God and He will see not our sin, but the holy righteousness of the Lord Jesus. This means that we are made righteous in the sight of God; that is, that we are accepted as righteous and treated as righteous by God on account of what the Lord Jesus has done. He was made sin; we are made righteousness" (Reference: https://www.gotquestions.org/righteousness.html/ What is Righteousness?).

- COVENANT: a contract or agreement between two parties. If we look at it biblically, God made several covenants between Him and His people. Two examples are: The Abrahamic Covenant, which was when God promised Abraham that he would be the father of a great nation and his name would be made great, and The New Covenant. "The New Covenant is a covenant made first with the nation of Israel and, ultimately, with all mankind. In the New Covenant, God promises to forgive sin, and there will be a universal knowledge of the Lord. Jesus Christ came to fulfill the Law of Moses (Matthew 5:17) and create a new covenant between God and His people. Now that we are under the New Covenant, both Jews and Gentiles can be free from the penalty of the Law. We are now given the opportunity to receive salvation as a free gift (Ephesians 2:8-9)" (Reference: https://www.gotquestions.org/bible-covenants.html/ What Are The Covenants in The Bible?).

- ANOINTING/ANOINTED: The meaning of these words is normally used when saying that someone is chosen by God to lead others to Him. People usually say, "He got that anointing on him." But the back story of this word and what it represents in Christianity now is so deep. Look at this— "The origin of anointing was from a practice of shepherds. Lice and other insects would often get into the wool of sheep, and when they got near the sheep's head, they could burrow into the sheep's ears and kill the sheep. So, ancient shepherds poured oil on the sheep's head. This made the wool slippery, making it impossible for insects to get near the sheep's ears because the insects would slide off. From this, anointing became symbolic of blessing, protection, and empowerment.... Another meaning for the word anointed is "chosen one." The Bible says that Jesus Christ was anointed by God with the Holy Spirit to spread the Good News and free those who have been held captive by sin (Luke 4:18-19; Acts 10:38). After Christ left the earth, He gave us the gift of the Holy Spirit (John 14:16). Now all Christians are anointed, chosen for a specific purpose in furthering God's Kingdom (1 John 2:20)" (Reference: https://www.gotquestions.org/anointed.html/ What is The Anointing?).

- ZEAL/ZEALOUS: "Zeal is often used in a religious sense, meaning **devotion to God or another religious cause**, like being a missionary" (Reference: https://www.vocabulary.com/dictionary/zeal). "Passionate ardor in the pursuit of anything. In general, zeal is an eagerness of desire to accomplish or obtain some object, and it may be manifested either in favor of any person or thing, or in opposition to it, and in a good or bad cause" (Reference: https://av1611.com/kjbp/kjv-dictionary/zeal.html).

- APOSTLE: I never knew there was a difference between these next two words, but come to find out, there is. Apostle is someone who is sent to fulfill some type of purpose (example: Paul was called by God to spread the Gospel to several different countries).

- DISCIPLE: A disciple is more like a student or a follower (example: Jesus' 12 disciples). "So the word apostle defines a person in terms of their purpose or mission, while disciple emphasizes the person's relationship to the teacher. In the case of the 12 apostles, all of them are disciples. But it doesn't follow that all disciples are apostles!" (Reference: https://www.bibleodyssey.org/en/tools/ask-a-scholar/apostles-vs-disciples/ Apostles vs. Disciples/ Jonathan Potter).

- GENTILE: anyone who is not a follower of Judaism/non-Jewish people.

- GRACE: These next two words I've had some difficulty understanding and knowing the difference between them. But I've heard my pastor put it like this. Grace is love that we don't deserve. "Grace is the opposite of karma, which is all about getting what you deserve. Grace is getting what you don't deserve, and *not* getting what you do deserve" (Reference: https://www.christianity.com/theology/what-is-grace.html/ What is Grace?/ Justin Holcomb).

- MERCY: While grace is getting what you don't deserve, mercy is not getting what you do deserve. Let that soak in a minute and really think about who God is based on these two definitions.

- TONGUES: "The first miraculous manifestation of the gift of tongues is described in Acts 2:1-4. To the amazement of the crowd in Jerusalem, the disciples were proclaiming the wonders of God in a language they had not learned. Knowing that the disciples were all Galileans, the people asked in amazement, 'And how is it that we hear, each of us in his own native language?' (Acts 2:7-11) The gift of speaking in languages unknown to the speaker was the outward sign that the Holy Spirit had now been given to all believers, just as Jesus had promised in John 14:15-20 and Acts 1:4-5. Tongues today are often a cause of confusion. Paul addresses this in 1 Corinthians 14:10: "There are doubtless many different languages in the world, and none is without meaning.' A 'tongue' without meaning is not a spiritual gift. Each of the gifts of the Spirit are given for the common good, so it doesn't stand to reason that a person would stand up in a worship service and speak unintelligibly 'for the common good' (1 Corinthians 12:7-11). Therefore, God gave the gift of interpretation of tongues alongside the gift of speaking in tongues"

(Reference: https://www.compellingtruth.org/speaking-in-tongues.html/ What is The Gift of Speaking in Tongues?).

- ATONEMENT: "Simply put, the word atonement means reconciliation. It refers to the condition of being one with others. More specifically, atonement is a reference to the sacrifice that Jesus Christ made in order to reconcile sinners to a holy God" (Reference: https://www.crosswalk.com/faith/bible-study/what-is-atonement-and-why-is-it-necessary.html/ What is Atonement and Why is it Necessary?/ Mike Leake). In the Old Testament, it was the priest's job to take all of the people's sacrifices and present them to God to restore the relationship between them and God (the book of Leviticus describes each one of these sacrifices. It is the book that explains the many rules that the people of Israel had to follow to be close to God). But now, it is Jesus who has restored the relationship we once had with our Father before the fall of Adam and Eve!

- TABERNACLE: "The Tabernacle of Ancient Israel was a sanctuary which was given in a vision to Moses as a pattern and constructed by the children of Israel. God's promise was that He would dwell within the Holy of Holies above the Mercy Seat of the Ark of the Covenant." (Reference: https://blogs.bible.org/impact/hal_warren/the_tabernacle_of_moses_%E2%80%93_god%E2%80%99s_heavenly_pattern_for_our_spiritual_transf ormation_part_ii/ The Tabernacle of Moses – God's Heavenly Pattern for our Spiritual Transformation - Part II: The Holy Place"/ Hal Warren).

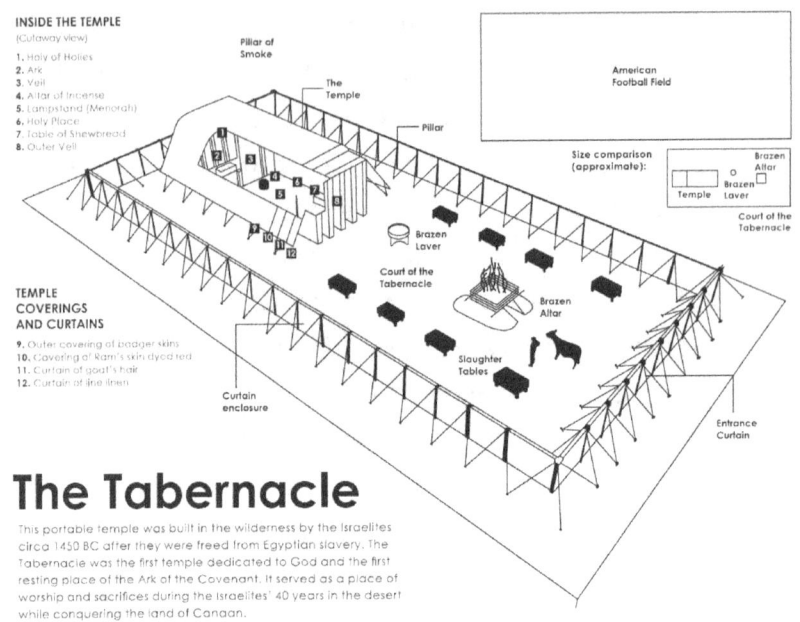

(Reference: https://i.pinimg.com/originals/95/d1/1c/95d11c3d1396c8bbb88ecd227e177fc2.jpg)

- COMMUNION: also called the Lord's Supper, is done to remember the death, burial, and resurrection of Jesus Christ. Normally, ushers will go around the church and pass out trays of crackers and little cups of grape juice. The grape juice represents the blood Jesus shed on the cross, and the crackers represent His body. It is something to be taken very seriously. It's not just eating a few crackers and drinking juice. Jesus speaks on taking communion until His return to take the church to Heaven in Matthew 26:26-29."This remembrance entails the use of ***tangible elements:*** bread and wine. It isn't enough simply to say, 'Remember!' The elements of bread and wine are given to stir our minds and hearts. The physical act of eating and drinking is designed to remind us that we spiritually 'ingest' and depend upon Jesus and the saving benefits of his life, death, and resurrection. Just as food and drink are essential to sustain physical existence, so also the blessings and benefits that come to us through the body and blood of Christ are paramount to our spiritual flourishing. In this remembering there is also ***confession***. In partaking of the elements we declare: 'Christ gave his body and blood for me. He died for me.' This is one among many reasons why I reject the practice of paedo-communion (the giving of the elements of the Table to infants). If one cannot and does not personally and consciously confess that the bread and wine symbolize the body and blood of Jesus sacrificed for sinners, he/she should not, indeed must not, partake of them" (Reference: https://www.crosswalk.com/faith/bible-study/10-things-you-should-know-about-the-lord-s-supper-from-1-corinthians.html,/ 10 Things You Should Know about the Lord's Supper and Communion/ Sam Storms).

- SELAH: this word is found mainly in the book of Psalms. There is no clear translation from Hebrew to English for this particular word, but this is what I've learned. "Perhaps the best way to think of *selah* is a combination of all these meanings. The Amplified Bible adds 'pause and calmly think about that' to each verse where *selah* appears. When we see the word *selah* in a psalm or in Habakkuk 3, we should pause to carefully weigh the meaning of what we have just read or heard, lifting up our hearts in praise to God for His great truths. 'All the earth bows down to you; they sing praise to you, they sing the praises of your name. *Selah!*' (Psalm 66:4)" (Reference: https://www.gotquestions.org/selah.html/ What Does *Selah* Mean in the Bible?).

- BRIDE OF CHRIST: that's us, the church! "The imagery and symbolism of marriage is applied to Christ and the body of believers known as the church. The church is comprised of those who have trusted in Jesus Christ as their personal Savior and have received eternal life. Christ, the Bridegroom, has sacrificially and lovingly chosen the church to be His bride (Ephesians 5:25–27). Just as there was a betrothal period in biblical times during which the bride and groom were separated until the wedding, so is the bride of Christ separate from her Bridegroom during the church age. Her responsibility during the betrothal period is to be faithful to Him (2 Corinthians 11:2; Ephesians 5:24). At the rapture, the church will be united with the Bridegroom and the official 'wedding ceremony' will take place and, with it, the eternal union of Christ and His bride will be actualized (Revelation 19:7–9; 21:1-2)." (https://www.gotquestions.org/bride-of-Christ.html, "What Does it Mean That The Church is the Bride of Christ?").

- FRUIT: the mental, spiritual, and emotional results of living a life of either pleasing your flesh or living to please Jesus Christ. Look at human beings as trees. Whatever our roots are grounded in, be it ourselves (our own selfish desires of the flesh) or Jesus Christ, the things that are growing from our branches (attitudes, mindsets, beliefs) are the fruit! Get it?
    - EXAMPLES OF FRUIT (TECHNICALLY KNOWN AS "WORKS") OF THE FLESH (GALATAINS 5:19-21):
        - Jealousy
        - Strife
        - Sexual immorality
        - Idolatry
    - FRUIT OF THE SPIRIT (GALATIANS 5:22-23):
        - Love
        - Patience
        - Kindness
        - Joy

- FAITHFULNESS: "Faithfulness is the concept of unfailingly remaining loyal to someone or something, and putting that loyalty into consistent practice regardless of extenuating circumstances" (Reference: https://en.wikipedia.org/wiki/Faithfulness).

- HALLEJUAH/ALLELUIA: "God be praised" (Reference: www.dictonary.com).

- RAPTURE: "The rapture is when Jesus Christ returns to remove the church (all believers in Christ) from the earth. The rapture is described in **1 Thessalonians 4:13-18** and **1 Corinthians 15:50-54**. Believers who have died will have their bodies resurrected and, along with believers who are still living, will meet the Lord in the air. This will all occur in a moment, in a twinkling of an eye" (Reference: https://www.gotquestions.org/difference-Rapture-Second-Coming.html/ What is the Difference Between the Rapture and the Second Coming?). Believers' bodies will also be changed to fit our eternal life ("We know that when he [Christ] appears, we shall be like him, for we shall see him as he is" (1 John 3:2). The movie "Left Behind" gives a pretty good illustration of what will happen on this day. This event occurs to usher in God's judgment against unbelievers. "After the Rapture, Christians will come before the Judgment Seat of Christ (**2 Corinthians 5:10**). The Judgment Seat is not about whether we will enter Heaven—we'll already be there because our sins have been atoned for in the substitutionary death and resurrection of Jesus Christ. It will, however, be a time to give an account of the works we have done on earth, and we will be rewarded accordingly. We'll be assigned places of authority in the coming Millennium based upon our faithfulness to God when we were on earth, as well as the influence we left behind" (Reference: https://www.crosswalk.com/faith/spiritual-life/4-things-every-christian-should-know-about-the-rapture.html/ 4 Things Every Christian Should Know about the Rapture/ Dr.

David Jeremiah). No one knows when it will happen; only God knows!

- TRIBULATION: Something you don't want to be around for. It will be a period of seven years of sheer torment and despair for the unbelievers left on Earth after the rapture. You can look in the book of Revelation and Daniel 9:24-27 for a complete description of what will happen. (I definitely wouldn't recommend reading it alone.) It requires a lot of study and research in order to really understand what it all means, but here are some of the main things that occur during the tribulation. I strongly encourage you to read up on it. The many signs that Jesus said to look out for before His return are beginning to occur, and it's time for people to get saved now before it is too late. I'll include some videos and websites that go into further detail about it.
    - "the beast" will emerge and command people to worship him. Anyone who refuses will be killed.
    - Four Horsemen of the Apocalypse. Each of these Horsemen will bring something into the Earth during the tribulation.
        - White Horse—Antichrist will bring 3 ½ years of peace and then 3 ½ years of war
        - Red Horse—war/bloodshed
        - Black Horse—famine.
        - Pale Horse—death

- REPENTANCE: the act of not only turning away from one's sin and asking God for forgiveness, but taking the steps to actually change your ways; not wanting to commit the sin again.

- PROVIDENCE: "It means 'to supply what is needed; to give sustenance or support.' And so the noun 'providence' has come to mean the act of 'providing for or sustaining and governing the universe by God.' What then is the providence of God? Here is the answer of the Heildelberg Catechism (Question 27): It is: The almighty and ever-present power of God, whereby, as it were, by his hand, he still upholds heaven and earth, with all creatures, and so governs them that herbs and grass, rain and drought, fruitful and barren years, meat and drink, health and sickness, riches and poverty, yea, all things come not by chance, but by his fatherly hand" (Reference: https://www.desiringgod.org/articles/the-providence-of-god/ The Providence of God: Seeing to The Universe/ John Piper).

- CONVICTION: "We are convicted when we become mindful of how much our sin dishonors God. When David was convicted by the Holy Spirit, he cried out, "Against you, you only, have I sinned and done what is evil in your sight" (Psalm 51:4). David saw his sin primarily as an affront to a holy God" (Reference: https://www.gotquestions.org/conviction-of-sin.html/ What is the Conviction of Sin?).

- CONDEMNATION: On the flip side, while conviction is received from the Holy Ghost, condemnation comes from our enemy. He loves to attack our minds with guilt and shame after we commit a sin or give into temptation. He likes to make us feel shameful for the mistakes we've made in the past, even when God has already forgiven them. Conviction is a loving way of God redirecting us, and condemnation is meant to make us feel low, useless and hopeless.

- SOVEREIGNTY: "God's 'sovereignty' means that He is absolute in authority and unrestricted in His supremacy. Everything that happens is, at the very least, the result of God's **permissive will**. This holds true, even if certain specific things are not what He would prefer. The right of God to allow mankind's free choices is just as necessary for true sovereignty as His ability to enact His will, wherever and however He chooses" (Reference: https://www.gotquestions.org/God-is-sovereign.html/What Does it Mean That God is Sovereign?). I suggest you read this article in its entirety because there are naturally going to be some questions that come up about God's sovereignty in relation to man's free will.

JEWISH HOLIDAYS AND HOLY DAYS RECOGNIZED IN OLD TESTAMENT

If you didn't know already, the Torah (Jewish Holy Book) is also the first few books of the Old Testament in the Bible. The people in the Old Testament (Israelites) followed specific laws that were given to Moses by God in order to maintain a relationship with God. These were the first people of the Jewish religion. Some Jewish people today (depending if they are Orthodox, Conservative, or Reform Jews) are still following the laws of the Torah and believe that they are still awaiting the coming of the Messiah. Christians accept the sacrifice that Jesus Christ offered on the cross, so they don't have to follow the laws of the Old Testament to have a relationship with God. I just wanted to go over what some of the Jewish holidays mentioned in the Bible are so we have a clearer meaning of each of them (look for more explanation of the connection between Judaism and Christianity in my next book).

- PASSOVER: the holiday where Jewish people remember two significant events that occurred in the Old Testament. In the book of Exodus, it tells the story of how the Hebrews were enslaved by the Egyptians and how God sent Moses to tell Pharaoh to free the Hebrews. When Pharaoh refused, God sent multiple plagues against Egypt, one of them being the killing of all the first-born Egyptian sons. The night before this plague, God spoke to Moses and told him to tell all the Hebrews to cover their doorways with sheep's blood and the angel of death would *pass over* their homes and their sons would not be harmed. During this holiday, Jewish people are to eat unleavened bread, or bread without yeast. This is because, following the angel of death plague, Pharaoh let the Hebrews go free and they didn't have enough time to make bread with yeast in it. They had to pack up what they could in a short amount of time. What I also didn't know was that there is a connection between this holiday and the resurrection of Jesus. "OT Israel looked back to the Exodus through the Passover meal. NT Israel (that's us) looks back to the cross and resurrection of Jesus through the Lord's Supper" (Reference: https://www.desiringgod.org/articles/the-ot-lords-supper-the-nt-passover/The OT Lord's Supper, the NT Passover/ Jon Bloom).

- ROSH HASHANAH: "Literally the 'head of the year,' Rosh Hashanah is one of four new year holidays designated in the Jewish calendar and the de facto 'Jewish New Year.' The first of the two High Holy Days listed in Leviticus (Yom Kippur being the second), Rosh Hashanah is at once a joyous celebration and a time of solemn reflection. Originally a 'memorial of blowing of trumpets,' Rosh Hashanah has by rabbinical tradition become a 'Day of Judgment.' The holiday—and the Ten Days of Awe that fall between it and Yom Kippur (the Day of Atonement)—provides us with an opportunity to make amends for past wrongs in preparation for the new year. In Leviticus 23: 23–25, the Lord establishes the Day of Trumpets (or the Feast of Trumpets): And the LORD spoke to Moses, saying, 'Speak to the people of Israel, saying, In the seventh month, on the first day of the month, you shall observe a day of solemn rest, a memorial proclaimed with blast of trumpets, a holy convocation. You shall not do any ordinary work, and you shall present a food offering to the

LORD.' This holy convocation formed the basis for what we now know as Rosh Hashanah. The sound of the trumpets reminded our people of the Lord's faithfulness thus far, rang in the year to come, and also hinted at the future coming of the Messiah." (Reference: https://jewsforjesus.org/jewish-resources/community/jewish-holidays/rosh-hashanah-the-jewish-new-year-and-feast-of-trumpets/Rosh Hashanah: The Jewish New Year and Feast of Trumpets).

- YOM KIPPUR (DAY OF ATONEMENT): "Yom Kippur, the Day of Atonement, is the holiest and most somber day of the Jewish year. Yom Kippur concludes the Ten Days of Awe that begin with Rosh Hashanah (the Jewish New Year). Like Rosh Hashanah, Yom Kippur is a prospective holiday, when we prepare for the year ahead through fasting, penitence and confession. Yom Kippur required action from both the high priest and the people—the high priest was to make atonement through sacrifice, and the people for their part were to practice self-denial and refrain from work. Thus, all Israelites had to do their part during this collective Day of Atonement. By God's commandment, the high priest followed a specific protocol on Yom Kippur. He bathed and dressed in white linen raiments, an act of purification, before entering the Holy of Holies. There the high priest made two sin offerings: a bull for his house and a goat for the people. The priest would lay the sins of the people on the head of a second goat, which had been chosen by lot as the 'scapegoat'. After the high priest spoke the sins and iniquities of the people and put them on its head, the scapegoat would be removed into the wilderness" (Reference: https://jewsforjesus.org/jewish-resources/community/jewish-holidays/yom-kippur/ Yom Kippur: A Day of Atonement).

- SABBATH: "According to Exodus 20:8–11, the Sabbath is the seventh day of the week, on which we are to rest, in remembrance that God created the universe in six days and then 'rested' on the seventh day. Traditionally, Christians have held their primary corporate worship services on Sundays, the first day of the week, in celebration of Christ's resurrection, which occurred on a Sunday (Matthew 28:1; Mark 16:2; Luke 24:1; John 20:1). It is important to understand, though, that Sunday is not the commanded day of corporate worship, either. There is no explicit biblical command that either Saturday or Sunday be the day of worship. Scriptures such as Romans 14:5–6 and Colossians 2:16 give Christians freedom to observe a special day or to observe every day as special. God's desire is that we worship and serve Him continually, every day, not just on Saturday or Sunday" (Reference: https://www.gotquestions.org/Sabbath-day-rest.html,/ What is The Sabbath Day?).

- HANUKAH: "The Feast of Dedication, which was once also called the Feast of the Maccabees, was an eight-day winter festival celebrated by the Jews in the month of December or sometimes late November, depending on when it fell in the lunisolar Jewish calendar. Today, this festival is called Hanukkah or the Festival of Lights. The history of the Feast of Dedication goes back to the intertestamental period and the Maccabean Revolt. After the Seleucid king Antiochus Ephiphanes profaned the Jewish temple and forced the Jews to abandon their sacrifices and adopt pagan rituals, a group of Jewish freedom fighters rose up, defied the oppressive pagan regime, and overthrew the Seleucids. The temple in Jerusalem was re-dedicated to God; ever since then, the Feast of Dedication has been celebrated to commemorate this meaningful event in Jewish history. The original Feast of Dedication involved a miracle, according to rabbinic tradition. When the Jews re-entered the temple they could only find one small, sealed jug of olive oil that had not been profaned or contaminated by the Seleucids. They used this to light the menorah in the temple, and though the oil was only enough to last one day, it miraculously lasted eight days—time for more oil to be made ready. This is the reason Hanukkah lasts for eight days" (Reference: https://www.gotquestions.org/Feast-of-Dedication.html/ What is The Feast of Dedication?).

CHRISTIAN HOLIDAYS EXPLAINED

- PALM SUNDAY: "Palm Sunday began with Jesus and His disciples traveling over the Mount of Olives. The Lord sent two disciples ahead into the village of Bethphage to find an animal to ride. They found the unbroken colt of a donkey, just as Jesus had said they would (Luke 19:29–30).

When they untied the colt, the owners began to question them. The disciples responded with the answer Jesus had provided: 'The Lord needs it" (Luke 19:31–34). Amazingly, the owners were satisfied with that answer and let the disciples go. 'They brought [the donkey] to Jesus, threw their cloaks on the colt and put Jesus on it' (Luke 19:35). As Jesus ascended toward Jerusalem, a large multitude gathered around Him. This crowd understood that Jesus was the Messiah; what they did not understand was that it wasn't time to set up the kingdom yet—although Jesus had tried to tell them so (Luke 19:11–12). The crowd's actions along the road give rise to the name 'Palm Sunday': 'A very large crowd spread their cloaks on the road, while others cut branches from the trees and spread them on the road' (Matthew 21:8). In strewing their cloaks on the road, the people were giving Jesus the royal treatment—King Jehu was given similar honor at his coronation (2 Kings 9:13). John records the detail that the branches they cut were from palm trees (John 12:13). On that first Palm Sunday, the people also honored Jesus verbally: 'The crowds that went ahead of him and those that followed shouted, 'Hosanna to the Son of David!' / 'Blessed is he who comes in the name of the Lord!' / 'Hosanna in the highest heaven!' (Matthew 21:9). In their praise of Jesus, the Jewish crowds were quoting Psalm 118:25–26, an acknowledged prophecy of the Christ" (Reference: https://www.gotquestions.org/Palm-Sunday.html,/ What is Palm Sunday?).

- GOOD FRIDAY: the day that Jesus Christ died on the cross. It's very ironic that we call it *"Good"* Friday, don't you think? We are the only religion that celebrates and benefits from someone's death.

- EASTER: three days after Good Friday (Sunday morning), Mary Magdalene and another Mary went to visit His tomb and found it empty! It was guarded by two Roman soldiers, so it wouldn't have been easy for Him to just escape. "Sitting on the rolled away stone was an angel of the Lord who told them to not be afraid because Jesus had risen. As the women left to tell the disciples, Jesus Christ met them and showed them his nail-pierced hands" (Reference: https://www.biblestudytools.com/bible-stories/the-easter-bible-story.html/ The Easter Bible Story).

- CHRISTMAS: the birth of Jesus. When Mary was still pregnant, there was a census that was being held and everyone was ordered to return to the town of their families' origin. This meant that Joseph and Mary had to travel to Bethlehem from Nazareth. A lot of us know the basis of the story. There was no room at any of the inns because of the census being held so Mary and Joseph had to sleep among animals. Three wise men followed a star that formed in the sky to mark Jesus' birth. They traveled all the way from Judea to Bethlehem with gifts for the new King of the Jews who had been born (frankincense, myrrh, and gold).

KEY PEOPLE IN THE BIBLE
- PAUL:
  - Born with the name Saul
    - "Paul was a Jew, born in the Roman city of Tarsus. He was proud of his Jewish heritage, as he describes in Philippians 3:5: Circumcised on the eighth day, of the race of Israel, of the tribe of Benjamin, a Hebrew of Hebrew parentage, in observance of the law a Pharisee." So zealous and devout was he that persecuting Christians was the natural way for him to show his devotion. He chose to use his Hebrew name, *Saul*, until sometime after he began to believe in and preach Christ. After that time, as 'the apostle to the Gentiles' (Romans 11:13), he used his Roman name, *Paul*. It would make sense for Paul to use his Roman name as he traveled farther and farther into the Gentile world" (Reference: https://www.gotquestions.org/Saul-Paul.html/ When and Why Was Saul's Name Changed to Paul?).
  - Pharisee.
  - Aided in the imprisonment and killing of Christians before becoming one himself.
  - Wrote most of the New Testament.
  - Named the greatest Apostle of all time.
  - Traveled to different countries sharing the Gospel.

- PETER:
  - Born with the name Simon/Simon Peter
    - Jesus gave him the name Peter, which means "rock". "It was Peter who declared that Jesus was "the Messiah, the Son of the living God" (Matthew 16:16). Jesus replied to him as 'Simon son of Jonah,' saying that he was blessed because God revealed Jesus' identity as Messiah to him. He then referred to him as 'Peter' and said that Peter's declaration was the basis, or 'rock,' on which He would build His church (Matthew 16:17–18)" (Reference: https://www.gotquestions.org/name-change.html/ Why Did God Sometimes Change a Person's Name in the Bible?).
  - "Peter was enthusiastic, strong-willed, impulsive, and, at times, brash" (Reference: https://www.gotquestions.org/life-Peter.html/ Who Was Peter in The Bible?). In short, he was *really* outspoken. "He was an outspoken and ardent disciple, one of Jesus' closest friends, an apostle, and a "pillar" of the church (Galatians 2:9)" (Reference: https://www.gotquestions.org/life-Peter.html/ Who Was Peter in The Bible?).
  - Denied he knew Jesus the night He was arrested (Jesus told him that he would do this beforehand, but Peter didn't believe Him). "Peter said to him, "Even though they all fall away, I will not." And

Jesus said to him, "Truly, I tell you, this very night, before the rooster crows twice, you will deny me three times." But he said emphatically, "If I must die with you, I will not deny you." And they all said the same." Mark 14: 29-31.
  - Was a fisherman along with two other disciples (James and John).
  - Was brothers with fellow disciple Andrew.

- JOB:
  - Man who was targeted by Satan (with God's permission) to attack him in various areas of his life.
    - Satan killed his children, gave him a disease, plus, he lost all his money and property.
  - Satan wanted to try and prove that Job would turn his back on God if he tormented him enough. Ultimately, in the end, Job didn't crack under the pressure and ended up being blessed with more children and money than he had before! There's a strong lesson here. Be faithful to God, no matter how big the fight. God will always restore what you have lost.

- GABRIEL: "The angel Gabriel is a messenger who was entrusted to deliver several important messages on God's behalf. Gabriel appears to at least three people in the Bible: first to the prophet Daniel (Daniel 8:16); next to the priest Zechariah to foretell and announce the miraculous birth of John the Baptist (Luke 1:19); and finally to the virgin Mary to tell her that she would conceive and bear a son (Luke 1:26–38). Gabriel's name means 'God is great,' and, as the angel of the annunciation, he is the one who revealed that the Savior was to be called 'Jesus' (Luke 1:31)" (Reference: https://www.gotquestions.org/angel-Gabriel.html/ What Does the Bible say About the Angel Gabriel?).

- MICHAEL: "Michael the archangel is described in the Bible, in the books of Daniel, Jude, and Revelation, as a warrior angel who engages in spiritual combat. The word archangel means 'angel of the highest rank.' Most angels in the Bible are portrayed as messengers, but Michael is described in all three books as contending, fighting, or standing against evil spirits and principalities (Daniel 10:13;21; Jude 1:9; Revelation 12:7). We do not have a full picture of any angel, and only two are named in the Bible (Gabriel is the other). Scripture only gives us hints of their movements during human events, but it is safe to say that Michael, the archangel, is a powerful being. Despite his great power, Michael is still in total submission to the Lord. His dependence on the Lord's power is seen in Jude 1:9. The righteous angels have a rank and are submissive to authority, and for this reason they are used as a picture of a wife's submission to her husband (1 Corinthians 11:10). Taking into consideration the strength of Michael, the archangel, his submission to God is all the more beautiful. If the submission of angels is an argument for woman's submission, we can see that submission is never meant to take away a woman's strength or purpose or value" (Reference: https://www.gotquestions.org/Michael-the-archangel.htm/ Who is Michael, The Archangel?). Read that last sentence again! I cannot wait to tackle that subject in the future.

- JUDAS ISACRIOT: The disciple who betrayed Jesus for thirty pieces of silver. He was asked by the Pharisees to show them who Jesus was.
    - Treasurer of the disciples.
    - "Judas was a common name in that era, and there are several other Judases mentioned in the New Testament. One of the other disciples was named Judas (John 14:22), and so was one of Jesus' own half-brothers (Mark 6:3). To differentiate, John 6:71 and John 13:26 refer to Christ's betrayer as 'Judas, son of Simon Iscariot.' Scholars have several ideas about the derivation of the surname. One is that *Iscariot* refers to Kerioth, a region or town in Judea. Another idea is that it refers to the Sicarii, a cadre of assassins among the Jewish rebels. The possible association with the Sicarii allows for interesting speculation about Judas' motives for his betrayal, but the fact that he made a conscious choice to betray Jesus (Luke 22:48) remains the same. The surname Iscariot is useful, if for no other reason, in that it leaves no doubt about which

Judas is being referred to" (Reference: https://www.gotquestions.org/Judas-Iscariot.html/ Who Was Judas Isacriot?).

- MARY: mother of Jesus Christ.
    - married to Joseph.
    - was a virgin until after Jesus' birth.

- MARY OF BETHANY, MARTHA, AND LAZARUS:
    - All of them were siblings.
    - The book of Luke tells the story of how Jesus came to visit their home. While Martha was running around trying to make sure that the house and meal were ready for Jesus and the disciples, Mary decided to sit at Jesus' feet and listen to everything He had to say.
    - We see the sisters again in the book of John when Jesus brings their brother, Lazarus, back from the dead.

- MARY MAGDELENE: "Mary Magdalene was a woman from whom Jesus cast out seven demons (Luke 8:2). The name Magdalene likely indicates that she came from Magdala, a city on the southwest coast of the Sea of Galilee. After Jesus cast seven demons from her, she became one of His followers" (Reference: https://www.gotquestions.org/Mary-Magdalene.html,/Who Was Mary Magdalene?).

- o Walked with Jesus as He carried His cross from Jerusalem to Galilee.
  - o Watched Him die on the cross.
  - o One of the first people at Jesus' tomb the morning of His resurrection.

- JOHN, THE BAPTIST:
  - o Jesus' cousin.
  - o Baptized Jesus.
  - o Killed for telling King Herod that divorcing his wife and marrying his brother's wife was sinful.
  - o "He was called 'The Baptist' because his practice was to baptize those who responded to the message he proclaimed and sincerely repented of their sins (Matthew 3:1 ; Mark 6:14; Luke 7:20)." (Reference: https://www.biblestudytools.com/dictionary/john-the-baptist/ John The Baptist).
  - o People thought that he was the Messiah they had been waiting for.
  - o "John's voice was a "lone voice in the wilderness" (John 1:23) as he proclaimed the coming of the Messiah to a people who desperately needed a Savior. He was the precursor for the modern-day evangelist as he unashamedly shared the good news of Jesus Christ. He was a man filled with faith and a role model to those of us who wish to share our faith with others. Most everyone, believer and non-believer alike, has heard of John the Baptist.

He is one of the most significant and well-known figures in the Bible. While John was known as "the Baptist," he was in fact the first prophet called by God since Malachi some 400 years earlier" (Reference: https://www.gotquestions.org/life-John-Baptist.html/ Who Was John The Baptist in The Bible?).

- ABRAHAM, ISSAC, ISHMAEL, JACOB, AND ESSAU (bear with me on the length of the next few people. A lot has to be said about them):
    - **Abraham**
        - the father of Israel. He was told by God Himself that he would be the father of many nations.
        - Had a child with his wife, Sarah, when he was 100 years old (Isaac).
        - Named Abram before being told of his purpose from God
            - Abram meant "high father" while Abraham means "father of multitude".
        - Was called by God to leave his homeland and follow His commands into a land he knew nothing of.
    - **Ishmael**
        - First child of Abraham. Mother was Hagar, Sarah's handmaid. "God had appeared to Abraham and promised that he would have

a son and that he would be the father of many nations (Genesis 15). However, as time went on, Abraham had no children. His wife, Sarah, had been unable to conceive, and they began to question just how the promise would be fulfilled. In Genesis 16 Sarah suggests that Abraham should have a child with her slave Hagar, an Egyptian. Apparently, this was a somewhat common practice at the time (also practiced in Genesis 30 by Jacob's wives): the wife would give a female slave to her husband, but any children born would be counted as the children of the wife (perhaps an ancient version of surrogacy). While this may have seemed like a workable solution for Abraham and Sarah, in actuality it caused more problems than it solved. Hagar did conceive a child with Abraham. When Hagar knew she was pregnant, she began to 'despise' Sarah, and Sarah appealed to Abraham for help. Abraham told Sarah to do as she saw fit, so she began to mistreat Hagar, and Hagar ran away (Genesis 16:4–6)" (Reference: https://www.gotquestions.org/Ishmael-in-the-Bible.html/ Who Was Ishmael in The Bible?).

- - "Ishmael is considered a patriarch of Islam based upon legends that have developed around him and information found in the Qur'an" (Reference: https://www.gotquestions.org/Ishmael-in-the-Bible.html,/ Who Was Ishmael in The Bible?).
  - **Isaac**
    - Second child of Abraham.
    - Abraham almost sacrificed him after God commanded him to do so in Genesis 22:1-19.
    - Married Rebekah and had twins Jacob and Esau.
  - **Jacob**
    - One of Abraham's grandsons.
    - One of Isaac and Rebekah's twin boys.
    - "Jacob's life began with a struggle. As a twin in the womb with Esau, he jostled for position and was born grasping his brother's heel. Jacob's name is translated as "he deceives" (Genesis 25:26). When his mother, Rebekah, asked God during her pregnancy what was happening to her, God told her that there were two nations within her womb who would become divided. One would be stronger than the other, and the older would serve the younger (Genesis 25:23). Jacob and Esau grew up together

living a nomadic life. Esau became a fine hunter and loved to be out in the countryside, while Jacob "was content to stay at home among the tents" (Genesis 25:27). Esau, being a hunter, was his father's favorite as Isaac loved the wild game Esau brought home, while Jacob was favored by his mother (Genesis 25:28). This destructive favoritism would follow the family into the next generation, most notably with Jacob's son Joseph. Such was Jacob's favoritism for Joseph that it caused great resentment among his brothers and nearly cost Joseph his life. When Isaac was old and his eyesight faded, he thought he was near to his death and made arrangements with Esau to pass on to him the blessings due to the firstborn son (Genesis 27:1-4). On hearing this, Rebekah devised a plan to deceive Isaac into blessing Jacob instead. Thus, Jacob received his father's blessing in Esau's place. Esau vowed he would kill Jacob for this as soon as the period of mourning for his father's death ended (Genesis 27:41). As it turned out, his father did not die for about another twenty years (Genesis 35:27–29). However, Rebekah became aware of Esau's plan and warned Jacob. Rebekah also told Isaac that

Jacob should find himself a wife from among his own people, so Isaac sent Jacob to his uncle Laban who lived in their ancestral home of Haran (Genesis 27:43). During Jacob's journey, he had a dream of a ladder to heaven with God at the top and angels ascending and descending. This imagery is mirrored in Jesus' words to His disciple Nathanael (John 1:51). God gave Jacob the assurance of His presence and reiterated His promise to Abraham (Genesis 28:13-15)"(Reference: https://www.gotquestions.org/life-Jacob.html/ Who Was Jacob in The Bible?).

- **Esau**
  - Esau was Abraham's grandson, the older twin born to Isaac and Rebekah (the younger was Jacob). "Rebekah had a difficult pregnancy, and God told her it was because 'two nations are in your womb; one people will be stronger than the other, and the older will serve the younger' (Genesis 25:23). Esau became a skillful hunter (Genesis 25:27), and his father favored him. His mother favored Jacob. Esau took his hunting seriously; one day he came in from hunting so tired and hungry that he thought he was going to die (our first indication that Esau was a whiner). His

hunger, along with the tantalizing scent of the red lentil stew his brother was cooking, convinced him to give up his birthright when Jacob asked for it (verses 29–34). Because of his desire for red stew, Esau became known as 'Edom,' which means 'red.' The son with the birthright would receive a double portion of the family inheritance, so Esau's giving up his birthright was a big deal. In order to fill his belly, Esau had 'despised his birthright' (verse 34). When Isaac neared the end of his life and was blind, he told Esau he wanted to bless him. Patriarchal blessings included encouragement and prophetic words about the future. Rebekah overheard her husband and told Jacob to pretend to be Esau so he could get Esau's blessing instead. While Esau was hunting and preparing food as Isaac had requested, Rebekah fixed Isaac's favorite recipe. She had Jacob wear Esau's clothes and put baby goat skin on his hands and neck so he'd feel hairy like Esau (Genesis 27:14–16). Jacob brought Isaac the meal and pretended he was Esau, telling his father a series of lies. Isaac believed him and gave Jacob a wonderful blessing that included a prophecy that he would be lord over his brother (verse 29). Later, when Esau brought his meal and Isaac realized Jacob had deceived him, Isaac was horrified (Genesis 27:33). Esau resorted to whining, pleading with his father for a blessing. Isaac couldn't find much to say except that Esau would eventually 'throw [Jacob's] yoke from off your neck' (verse 40). This prophecy was fulfilled when Esau's descendants revolted against Jacob's descendants (2 Kings 8:20). Bitterness filled Esau, and he vowed to kill Jacob after their father died (verse 41). Rebekah heard about the plan and intervened, telling Jacob to move away. Years later, when Jacob returned to Canaan, he feared Esau might try to kill him and his children. So he sent a lavish gift ahead of him and asked God to save him (Genesis 32:9–15). But he was wrong about Esau: 'Esau ran to meet Jacob and embraced him; he threw his arms around his neck and kissed him. And they wept' (Genesis 33:4). The men couldn't live in the same area because God had blessed them both so much with children, possessions, and livestock, so Esau moved to the hill country of Seir, an area south of the Dead Sea (Genesis 36:7–8). In spite of the fact that the brothers made peace,

Esau's descendants, the Edomites (also called Idumeans), never got along with Jacob's descendants, the Israelites. Edom regularly opposed and fought against Israel. A big part of the problem was that the Edomites were pagans and the Israelites followed God. The prophets Jeremiah and Obadiah said God would 'bring disaster on Esau' (Jeremiah 49:8) and that the Edomites would be eventually destroyed (Obadiah 1:18)" (Reference: https://www.gotquestions.org/Esau-in-the-Bible.html/ Who Was Esau in The Bible?).

- DAVID:
    - Called "a man after God's own heart".
    - Very passionate.
    - Was first a shepherd, then became King of Israel.
    - Killed Goliath (giant Philistine soldier) with a slingshot and a stone when he was young.
    - Wrote the book of Psalms.
    - Slept with another man's wife (Bathsheba) and had him killed so he could have her.

- CAIN AND ABEL:
    - First murder in the Bible.
    - Cain murdered Abel because of his anger and jealousy. "When it was time to offer sacrifices to God, Cain brought fruit from the ground and Abel

brought the fat portions from some of the firstborn. God favored Abel's sacrifice, but He didn't extend that same grace to Cain. This rejection made Cain angry and God admonished Cain to do the right thing and his sacrifice would be accepted. Cain was also warned that if he refused to do the right thing—sin was ready to consume him. Cain disregarded God's admonition and warning. Instead, he took out his anger on his righteous brother, Abel. In a premeditated manner, Cain invited Abel out to the fields where he murdered him! Later God approached Cain about the whereabouts of Abel just as He did with Adam and Eve with their sin. Cain (being a child of sin and the devil) lied and countered the all-knowing God with the infamous question, 'Am I my brother's keeper?' God responded quickly with the pronouncement of his punishment: Cain would be driven from his people, no longer able to farm the land and he would be a wanderer. Cain's response lacked remorse for his dead brother, but rather that his punishment was too severe and that he would be killed in revenge. The Lord God, being full of mercy and grace, put a mark on Cain to keep people from killing him. As a result Cain left the presence of God, started a family, and built a city. His descendants were prosperous, worldly, and without God. The legacy of Cain led to the destruction of the entire world with the flood"

(Reference: https://www.whatchristianswanttoknow.com/cain-and-abel-bible-story-summary/#ixzz5ZFI7tNuE/ Cain and Abel: A Bible Story Summary/ Crystal McDowell).

- 12 DISCIPLES:
  these were the people that Jesus chose to keep close as He preached. After speaking with the large crowds in His parables ("a simple story used to illustrate a moral or spiritual lesson, as told by Jesus in the Gospels" (Reference: www.dictionary.com). He would go into further detail and explain to them exactly what He meant. He was leading them so that after His resurrection, they would be able to spread the Gospel to different countries. Ultimately, most of them were killed for doing so.

    - PETER:
      look back a few paragraphs to get a refresher
        - Was also a follower of John the Baptist
        - older brother to Andrew
        - only disciple who was married
        - Asked to be crucified upside down because he didn't feel worthy to be crucified the same way as Jesus. "He died a martyr's death in Rome during the reign of Nero. Some speculate around the same time as Paul was being beheaded." (Reference: https://www.crosswalk.com/faith/bible-

study/who-were-the-12-disciples-and-what-should-we-know-about-them.html/ Who Were the 12 Disciples and What Should We Know about Them?/ Allyson Holland).

- ANDREW:
    - First to follow Jesus, introduced his older brother, Peter, to Him.
    - "Went to the 'land of the man-eaters,' in what is now the Soviet Union. Christians there claim him as the first to bring the gospel to their land. He also preached in Asia Minor, modern-day Turkey, and in Greece, where he is said to have been crucified" (Reference: https://www.christianity.com/church/church-history/timeline/1-300/whatever-happened-to-the-twelve-apostles-11629558.html,/ Whatever Happened to the Twelve Apostles?).

- JAMES (SON OF ZEBEDEE):
    - Older brother of fellow disciple, John (not John the Baptist).
    - "As part of Jesus' 'inner three' he was permitted to be present along with Peter and John when Jesus raised Jairus' daughter from the dead *(Mark 5:37)*, he witnessed Jesus' transfiguration on the Mount of

Olives *(Matthew 17:1)*, and he was in the Garden of Gethsemane with Jesus. *(Mark 14:33)* James was the first disciple to be martyred (he was beheaded) and the only disciple to have their martyrdom recorded in Scripture. *(Acts 12:1-3)"* (Reference: https://www.crosswalk.com/faith/bible-study/who-were-the-12-disciples-and-what-should-we-know-about-them.html/ Who Were the 12 Disciples and What Should We Know about Them?/ Allyson Holland)
- "...this James is reckoned to have ministered in Syria. The Jewish historian Josephus reported that he was stoned and then clubbed to death" (Reference: https://www.christianity.com/church/church-history/timeline/1-300/whatever-happened-to-the-twelve-apostles-11629558.html/ Whatever Happened to the Twelve Apostles?).

- JOHN:
  - Known as "the disciple who Jesus loved"
    - rested his head Jesus' chest at the Last Supper
    - part of Jesus' "inner three"
  - only disciple who was killed (died of natural causes)

- wrote the book of Revelation while on the island of Patmos in exile
- "He was exiled to the island of Patmos under Domitian, but after his death, John was allowed to return to Ephesus where he governed churches in Asia until his death at about A.D. 100" (Reference: https://www.crosswalk.com/faith/bible-study/who-were-the-12-disciples-and-what-should-we-know-about-them.html/ Who Were the 12 Disciples and What Should We Know about Them?/ Allyson Holland).

- PHILLIP:
    - "What do we know about Philip? Almost nothing. Although a Jew, we only know him by his Greek name, **Philip**. A heart for evangelism, he was anxious to tell Nathanael the One foretold by Moses and the prophets had been found. *(John 1:45)* They were close companions and possibly studied the Old Testament together. Philip was stoned and crucified in Hierapolis, Phrygia" (Reference: https://www.crosswalk.com/faith/bible-study/who-were-the-12-disciples-and-what-should-we-know-about-them.html/ Who Were the 12 Disciples and What Should We Know about Them?/ Allyson Holland).

- "...possibly had a powerful ministry in Carthage in North Africa and then in Asia Minor, where he converted the wife of a Roman proconsul. In retaliation the proconsul had Philip arrested and cruelly put to death" (Reference: https://www.christianity.com/church/church-history/timeline/1-300/whatever-happened-to-the-twelve-apostles-11629558.html/ Who Were the 12 Disciples and What Should We Know about Them?/ Allyson Holland).

- MATTHEW:
  - Tax collector.
    - Most people hated them because they were known to take extra money from tax payers and pocket it for themselves.
  - "Matthew brought the gospel to Ethiopia and Egypt. Hircanus the king had him killed with a **spear**." (Reference: https://www.crosswalk.com/faith/bible-study/who-were-the-12-disciples-and-what-should-we-know-about-them.html/ Who Were the 12 Disciples and What Should We Know about Them?/ Allyson Holland).

- NATHANAEL/BARTHOLOMEW:
    - "…came from Cana in Galilee. *(John 21:2)* He expressed some local prejudice about Nazareth. *(John 1:46)* Jesus recognized how sincerely his love for God was from the beginning when He said, *'Behold, an Israelite indeed, in whom there is no deceit!'* *(John 1:47)*. Nathanael may have preached in India and translated the book of Matthew into their language. He was beaten, crucified, and beheaded. He died as a martyr while serving the people of Albinopolis, Armenia" (Reference: https://www.crosswalk.com/faith/bible-study/who-were-the-12-disciples-and-what-should-we-know-about-them.html/ Who Were the 12 Disciples and What Should We Know about Them?/ Allyson Holland).

- THOMAS:
    - Nicknamed "Doubting Thomas"
        - Known for questioning if Jesus really resurrected.
    - "…was probably most active in the area east of Syria. Tradition has him preaching as far east as India, where the ancient Marthoma Christians revere him as their founder. They claim that he died there when pierced through with the spears of four soldiers"

(Reference: https://www.christianity.com/church/church-history/timeline/1-300/whatever-happened-to-the-twelve-apostles-11629558.html/ Whatever Happened to the Twelve Apostles?).

- SIMON THE ZEALOT:
  - "ministered in Persia and was killed after refusing to sacrifice to the sun god" (Reference: https://www.christianity.com/church/church-history/timeline/1-300/whatever-happened-to-the-twelve-apostles-11629558.html/ Whatever Happened to the Twelve Apostles?).
  - "Simon was probably a political activist in his younger years. Why would Jesus choose someone with this background? 'It is amazing that Jesus would select a man like Simon to be an apostle. But he was a man of fierce loyalties, amazing passion, courage, and zeal. Simon had believed the truth and embraced Christ as his Lord. The fiery enthusiasm he once had for Israel was now expressed in his devotion to Christ.' -Twelve Ordinary Men by John MacArthur. There is some speculation about what happened to Simon. Tradition says that

after preaching on the west coast of Africa, Simon went to England where he ended up being crucified in 74 AD" (Reference: https://www.crosswalk.com/faith/bible-study/who-were-the-12-disciples-and-what-should-we-know-about-them.html/ Who Were the 12 Disciples and What Should We Know about Them?/ Allyson Holland).

- JAMES (SON OF ALPHAEUS/JAMES THE LESS): "the son of Alpheus, is one of at least three James referred to in the New Testament. There is some confusion as to which is which, but this James is reckoned to have ministered in Syria. The Jewish historian Josephus reported that he was stoned and then clubbed to death" (Reference: https://www.christianity.com/church/church-history/timeline/1-300/whatever-happened-to-the-twelve-apostles-11629558.html/ Whatever Happened to the Twelve Apostles?).

- JUDAS (NOT JUDAS ISCARIOT):
    - Also known as Thaddeus
    - "Most early tradition says that Judas, son of James, a few years after Pentecost, took the gospel north to Edessa. There he healed the King of Edessa, Abgar. Eusebius the historian said the archives at Edessa contained the visit of Judas and the healing

of Abgar (the records have now been destroyed). The traditional symbol of Judas is a club and tradition says he was clubbed to death for his faith" (Reference: https://www.crosswalk.com/faith/bible-study/who-were-the-12-disciples-and-what-should-we-know-about-them.html/ Who Were the 12 Disciples and What Should We Know about Them?/ Allyson Holland).

- JUDAS ISCARIOT: Take a look back a few pages to get a refresher
  - "The other eleven apostles are all great encouragements to us because they exemplify how common people with typical failings can be used by God in uncommon, remarkable ways. Judas, on the other hand, stands as a warning about the evil potential of spiritual carelessness, squandered opportunity, sinful lusts, and hardness of the heart. Here was a man who drew as close to the Savior as it is humanly possible to be. He enjoyed every privilege Christ affords. He was intimately familiar with everything Jesus taught. Yet he remained in unbelief and went into a hopeless eternity." Twelve Ordinary Men by John MacArthur (Reference: https://www.crosswalk.com/faith/bible-

study/who-were-the-12-disciples-and-what-should-we-know-about-them.html/ Who Were the 12 Disciples and What Should We Know about Them?/, Allyson Holland).
  - Betrayed Jesus with a kiss. He revealed His idea identity to the Pharisees by kissing His cheek and calling Him "Rabbi".

- 12 TRIBES OF ISRAEL: the tribes were formed by the 12 children Jacob had with his two wives, Leah and Rachel. There is a whole messy backstory to how these 12 children came about....Jacob went back and forth having children between the two sisters Leah and Rachel, PLUS their handmaidens!! At first, Jacob fell in love with Rachel and the night after they were married, her father tricked him and gave him Leah, Rachel's older sister instead. "Jacob showed favoritism to Rachael and loved her more than Leah. God compensated for the lack of love Leah received by enabling her to have children and closing Rachel's womb for a time (Genesis 29:31). There developed an intense rivalry between the two wives. In fact, at one time the wives bartered over the right to sleep with Jacob. Genesis 30:16 says, 'When Jacob came from the field in the evening, Leah went out to meet him and said, 'You must come in to me, for I have hired you with my son's mandrakes.' So he lay with her that night,' and Leah became pregnant. In the end, Jacob fathered twelve sons and a daughter. Jacob and Leah had six sons and a daughter; Zilpah, Leah's maidservant, bore Jacob two sons;

Jacob and Rachel had two sons together; and Bilhah, Rachel's maidservant, bore Jacob another two sons (Genesis 35:23–36)" (Reference: https://www.gotquestions.org/Jacob-Leah-Rachel.html/ What is the Story of Jacob, Leah, and Rachel?). Here's the list of them from oldest to youngest...
- Reuben
- Simeon
- Levi (this priestly tribe did not receive a territory, and sometimes is not listed when the tribe of Joseph is listed as two separate tribes).
- Judah
- Zebulun
- Issachar
- Dan
- Gad
- Asher
- Naphtali
- Joseph (often listed as two tribes named for his sons, Ephraim and Manasseh)
- Benjamin

(Reference: https://lifehopeandtruth.com/prophecy/12-tribes-of-israel/the-12-tribes-of-israel/ The 12 Tribes of Israel in History and Prophecy/David Treybig)

- RACHEL: One of the two wives of Jacob. Jacob worked for her father, Laban, for seven years in order to win her hand in marriage. Between her and her sister, Leah (who Jacob was tricked into marrying), Jacob loved Rachel the most.

- SARAH:
    - Wife of Abraham.
    - Had a son (Isaac) at the age of 98.
    - Laughed at God when He told her and Abraham that they would have a son in their old age.
    - Said to be the most beautiful woman in all of the Bible.

- ESTHER: "Esther is the Jewish maiden who became queen of Persia and rescued her people from a murderous plot to annihilate them. Her story is recorded in the Old Testament book bearing her name. The Jewish Feast of Purim celebrates this particular deliverance of the Jews" (Reference: https://www.gotquestions.org/life-Esther.html/ Who Was Esther in The Bible?).
    - Also the only book in the Bible where God is not mentioned.

- HEBREWS/ISRAELITES:
    - Same people.
    - Called the Israelites because they are descendants from Jacob (renamed Israel in the Bible by God).
    - Called Hebrews by outside nations because this was the language they all spoke.

KEY PLACES IN THE BIBLE
- GALILIEE:
    - Region in northern Israel.
    - Towns in this region are Nazareth and Capernaum.

- - Sea of Galilee.
    - Freshwater lake.
    - Where Jesus called Peter, Andrew, James and John to be fishers of men.
    - Feeding of the 5000 and Sermon of the Mount occurred here.
    - Where Jesus walked on water and calmed the storm at sea (Reference: http://www.aboutbibleprophecy.com/s5.htm/ Galilee).

- ZION: "The first instance of the word Zion in the Bible is in 2 Samuel, and says, 'David took the stronghold of Zion, that is, the city of David' (2 Samuel 5:7). We can gather from this and other similar verses (1 Kings 8:1; 1 Chronicles 11:5; 2 Chronicles 5:2) that Zion and the City of David are meant to be synonymous. The Davidic Covenant, which prophesies the greatness of Solomon's rule, also prophesies that an Eternal Kingdom will come from David's line (2 Samuel 7:12-16). When Zion is mentioned in subsequent passages, it carries a spiritual, eternal meaning —just as King David was a temporal version of the eternal King, Jesus Christ, the 'city of David' was a temporal shadow of the eternal and spiritual city, Zion, where Christ will reign. Zion is described in the Psalms as 'the City of our God' and a place that belongs to Him. Situated on a high mountain, it is called 'the joy of all the earth' and 'the perfection of beauty' (Psalm 48; 50:2). It is the city that God will 'establish forever' and from which the kings of other nations will flee in panic (Psalm 48:4-8). Because of these descriptions, it is rational to assume that Zion is the location of Christ's rule on earth during the millennial kingdom(Revelation 12:5; Revelation 20:4-6; Psalm 69:35). Repeatedly, when the nation of Israel is favored or promised future glory, Zion is mentioned (Psalm 102:16; Psalm 99:2; Psalm 126:1; Psalm 128:5). Zion is the place from which 'the Lord has commanded the blessing, life forevermore' (Psalm 133:3). Zion can be thought of as the spiritual and future eternal Jerusalem (Isaiah 28:16; Isaiah 33:20). 'And the ransomed of the Lord shall return and come to Zion with singing; everlasting joy shall be upon their heads; they shall obtain gladness and joy, and sorrow and sighing shall flee away' (Isaiah 35:10). Zion is contrasted with Babylon, the place of exile (Psalm 137:1) where their captors taunted them, saying 'sing us one of the songs of Zion!' (Psalm 137:3). Just as Zion is both a real and a spiritual place, Babylon is its opposite: a real place that has a symbolic, spiritual counterpart as the persecutor of God's people and a city of evil (Revelation 18:1-24). Mount Zion, the physical place, is on a hill just outside of Jerusalem's wall. It has been associated with the Temple Mount, but also with the western hill. The entire land of Israel has also been referred to as Mount Zion" (Reference: https://www.compellingtruth.org/Zion.html/ What is the Biblical Significance of Zion? What is Zion? What is Mount Zion?).

- JERUSALEM:
    - "Jerusalem is called by various names in Scripture: 'Salem,' 'Ariel,' 'Jebus,' the 'city of God,' the 'holy city,' the 'city of David,' and 'Zion.' *Jerusalem* itself means "possession of peace" (Reference: https://www.gotquestions.org/city-of-Jerusalem.html, "What is the Significance of the City of Jerusalem?").
    - Considered a holy place to Jews, Muslims, and Christians
    - Where Jesus held the Last Supper, got arrested (Garden of Gethsemane) died on the cross (Golgotha) and rose again
    - Where Jesus performed healing miracles and preached
    - Where Jesus chased merchants out of the Temple (Matthew 21:12-17, Mark 11:15–19, and Luke 19:45–48).

- BETHLEHEM:
    - Where Jesus was born.
        - "It is written in Micah 5:2 that Bethlehem would be the birthplace of a future king of ancient origins. This prophecy was fulfilled with the birth of Jesus about 2000 years ago."
    - "During pre-Christian times, it was the home of Ruth and Boaz and their great grandson, David." (Reference:

http://www.aboutbibleprophecy.com/s1.htm/ Bethlehem)

- **CAPERNAUM:**
    - Where Jesus lived during his years of preaching.
    - "Peter, Andrew, James and John were fishermen living in the village. Matthew the tax collector also dwelt here" (Reference: https://www.bibleplaces.com/capernaum/ Capernaum).

- **NAZARETH:**
    - Where Jesus lived as a child.
    - Jesus returned here twice after living in Capernaum but was rejected twice. "On one occasion the townspeople were so outraged at Jesus that they tried to throw him off a cliff to his death" (Reference: https://www.bibleplaces.com/nazareth/ Nazareth).

- **MOUNT SINAI:**
    - Where God gave Moses the Ten Commandments.

- **SODOM AND GOMORRAH:**
    - Two cities destroyed due to their complete lack of fear of God and continuous sinning. Specifically, sexual sin. "While Sodom and Gomorrah were guilty of many other horrendous sins, homosexuality was the reason God poured fiery

sulfur on the cities, completely destroying them and all of their inhabitants. To this day, the area where Sodom and Gomorrah were located remains a desolate wasteland" (Reference: https://www.gotquestions.org/Sodom-and-Gomorrah.html/ What Was The Sin of Sodom and Gomorrah?).

- MOUNT CARMEL:
    - "Biblically, Mt. Carmel is referenced most often as a symbol of beauty and fertility" (Reference: https://www.bibleplaces.com/mtcarmel/ Mount Carmel).
    - This is where God showed His almighty power against the false, pagan gods of King Ahab. "After Israel had gone more than three years without rain as a judgment for their idolatry, the prophet Elijah confronts the evil king Ahab and challenges him to a spiritual showdown. The king was to have all Israel gather at Mt. Carmel, along with the 450 prophets of the false god **Baal and the 400 prophets of the false goddess Asherah** (verse 19)" (Reference: https://www.gotquestions.org/Elijah-prophets-Baal.html/ What is the Story of Elijah and the Prophets of Baal?).

- ISRAEL (12 TRIBES/LOCATIONS):
(Reference: https://www.biblestudy.org/maps/division-of-promised-land-to-twelve-tribes-israel.html)

- BABYLON:
  - Where the Tower of Babel was located.
    - The people of Babylon built it to try and represent their "power"
  - Ruled by King Nebuchadnezzar.
  - Known to be a city that rebelled against God.
    - "After the Flood, God commanded humanity to 'increase in number and fill the earth' (Genesis 9:1). Humanity decided to do the exact opposite, 'Then they said, 'Come, let us build ourselves a city, with a tower that reaches to the heavens, so that we may make a name for ourselves and not be scattered over the face of the whole earth' (Genesis 11:4). Humanity decided to build a great city and all congregate there."... "In response, God confused the languages of humanity so that they could no longer communicate with each other (Genesis 11:7). The result was that people congregated with other people who spoke the same language, and then went together and settled in other parts of the world (Genesis 11:8-9). God confused the languages at the Tower of Babel to enforce His command for humanity to spread throughout the entire world." "The Tower of Babel account, told in Genesis 11:1-9, is a "flashback" to the point in Genesis 10 when

the languages were confused. Genesis 10 tells us of different languages. Genesis 11 tells us how the different languages originated" (Reference: https://www.gotquestions.org/Tower-of-Babel.html/ What Happened at the Tower of Babel?).

- CANAAN:
    - "Canaan is described in the Bible as extending from Lebanon toward the Brook of Egypt in the south and the Jordan River Valley in the east. In the Bible, notably in Genesis 10 and Numbers 34, this was called the 'land of Canaan' and occupies the same area that is occupied by modern Lebanon and Israel, plus parts of Jordan and Syria."
    - "The land of Canaan was the land God promised to give to Abraham's descendants (Genesis 12:7)."
    - "The Canaanites are mentioned over 150 times in the Bible. They were a wicked, idolatrous people descended from Noah's grandson Canaan, who was a son of Ham (Genesis 9:18). Canaan was cursed because of his and his father's sin against Noah (Genesis 9:20–25). In some passages, *Canaanites* specifically refers to the people of the lowlands and plains of Canaan (Joshua 11:3); in other passages, *Canaanites* is used more broadly to refer to all the inhabitants of the land, including the Hivites, Girgashites, Jebusites, Amorites, Hittites, and

Perizzites (see Judges 1:9–10)" (Reference: https://www.gotquestions.org/Canaanites.html/ Who Were the Canaanites?)

- JERICHO:
    - "After the death of Moses, God chose Joshua, son of Nun, to be the leader of the Israelite people. They set about to conquer the land of Canaan, under the Lord's guidance. God said to Joshua: "Do not be terrified; do not be discouraged, for the Lord your God will be with you wherever you go." (Joshua 1:9, NIV). (Reference: https://www.thoughtco.com/battle-of-jericho-700195/ Battle of Jericho Bible Story/ Jack Zavada) Jericho was the first city God led the Israelites to conquer in Canaan.
    - the strongest fortress in all the land of Canaan. It was the key to Western Palestine. (Reference: https://www.biblestudytools.com/dictionary/jericho/ Jericho).
    - "Scouts from the Israelites crept into the walled city of Jericho and hid at the house of Rahab, noted as a prostitute. Rahab had faith in God and informed the Israelites of Jericho's fear saying "I know that the Lord has given you this land and that a great fear of you has fallen on us, so that all who live in this country are melting in fear because of you." She helped the scouts hide from the king's soldiers, then leave out a window since her house

was located next to the city wall. Rahab demanded the spies affirm an oath as she swore not to give their plans away, and congruently, they vowed to spare Rahab and her family when the battle of Jericho occurred. She was to fasten a scarlet rope in her window as the symbol of their protection" (Reference: https://www.biblestudytools.com/bible-stories/battle-of-jericho-bible-story.html/ Jericho).
  - At the Battle of Jericho, Joshua led the Israelites around the walls of Jericho for six days. On the last day, they walked around the wall, blew trumpets and shouted, and the walls crumbled, allowing them to gain control of the city.

- **JORDAN RIVER:**
  - "The Jordan River is a 156-mile-long river that flows north to south from the Sea of Galilee to the Dead Sea. It lies on the eastern border of modern-day Israel and the western borders of both Syria and Jordan. Because of its great length and central location, the Jordan River is mentioned in the Bible over 185 times."
  - "Here are some of the more well known instances where people of the Bible have come across the Jordan River:
    - Where John the Baptist preached and baptized people, including Jesus in the New Testament.

- The Israelites had to cross the river in order to get into the Promised Land. "Only the Jordan River stood in their way now, and it was at flood stage (Joshua 3:15). At God's command, Joshua (the people's new leader) instructed the priests bearing the Ark of the Covenant to stand in the water of the river. They obeyed, and the Jordan immediately stopped flowing to make a way for the people to cross over on dry ground (Joshua 3:15–17)."
- The Old Testament mentions the Jordan River many more times, usually in stories of the Israelites' battles and disputes." (Reference: https://www.gotquestions.org/Jordan-River.html/ What is the Significance of the Jordan River in the Bible?)

- THE PROMISED LAND: "According to Genesis 15:18 and Joshua 1:4, the land God gave to Israel included everything from the Nile River in Egypt to Lebanon (south to north) and everything from the Mediterranean Sea to the Euphrates River (west to east). So, what land has God stated belongs to Israel? All of the land modern Israel currently possesses, plus all of the land of the Palestinians (the West Bank and Gaza), plus some of Egypt and Syria, plus all of Jordan, plus some of Saudi Arabia and Iraq. Israel currently possesses only a fraction of the land God has promised" (Reference: https://www.gotquestions.org/Israel-land.html/ What is the Land That God Promised to Israel).

- HEAVEN: The definition of this place is a little more complex than I thought. It's a whole lot more than a place in the sky filled with clouds and angels.
    - "Scripture refers to three heavens. The apostle Paul was 'caught up to the third heaven,' but he was prohibited from revealing what he experienced there (2 Corinthians 12:1-9). If a third heaven exists, there must also be two other heavens. The first is most frequently referred to in the Old Testament as the 'sky' or the 'firmament.' This is the heaven that contains clouds, the area that birds fly through. The second heaven is interstellar/outer space, which is the abode of the stars, planets, and other celestial objects (Genesis 1:14-18). The third heaven, the location of which is not revealed, is the dwelling place of God. Jesus promised to prepare a place for true Christians in heaven (John 14:2). Heaven is also the destination of Old Testament saints who died trusting God's promise of the Redeemer (Ephesians 4:8). Whoever believes in Christ shall never perish but have eternal life (John 3:16). The apostle John was privileged to see and report on the heavenly city (Revelation 21:10-27). John witnessed that heaven (the new earth) possesses the 'glory of God' (Revelation 21:11), the

very presence of God. Because heaven has no night and the Lord Himself is the light, the sun and moon are no longer needed (Revelation 22:5). The city is filled with the brilliance of costly stones and crystal clear jasper. Heaven has twelve gates (Revelation 21:12) and twelve foundations (Revelation 21:14). The paradise of the Garden of Eden is restored: the river of the water of life flows freely and the tree of life is available once again, yielding fruit monthly with leaves that "heal the nations" (Revelation 22:1-2). However eloquent John was in his description of heaven, the reality of heaven is beyond the ability of finite man to describe (1 Corinthians 2:9). Heaven is a place of 'no mores.' There will be no more tears, no more pain, and no more sorrow (Revelation 21:4). There will be no more separation, because death will be conquered (Revelation 20:6). The best thing about heaven is the presence of our Lord and Savior (1 John 3:2). We will be face to face with the Lamb of God who loved us and sacrificed Himself so that we can enjoy His presence in heaven for eternity" (Reference: https://www.gotquestions.org/heaven-like.html/ What is Heaven Like?).

- HELL: Where anyone who doesn't accept Jesus as their Savior will spend eternity. It is a place of punishment as a result of the sin that people have committed in the world.

It is a place where God's presence does not exist. In the Bible, it is said to be a place of fire that never goes out, torment, and forever "living" with the knowledge of you refusing to accept God's invitation of salvation (Matthew 13:50, 2 Thessalonians 1:9). Hell was actually first created to punish Satan and his demons. Contrary to popular belief, the devil IS NOT the ruler of Hell. He is the ruler of this Earth and resides here. He will be thrown into Hell after the second coming of Jesus Christ.

COMMON CHURCH PHRASES AND SCRIPTURES EXPLAINED

- "BLESS THE LORD": I always wondered, how do you bless the Lord? Isn't He supposed to bless us? He's God; why would He need blessing, and how can we, as humans, bless an almighty God? "The phrases 'bless the Lord' and 'bless God' are found primarily in the Old Testament. The Psalms, especially, are filled with the psalmists' blessings upon God. The King James Version uses 'bless the Lord' many times, but the more modern translations render it 'praise the Lord.' The Hebrew word translated 'bless' or 'praise' means literally 'to kneel', the implication being to kneel in worship. Therefore, to bless the Lord means to praise Him, exalt Him and worship Him" (Reference: https://www.gotquestions.org/bless-God.html/ What Does It Mean to Bless God?).

- "FISHERS OF MEN": Jesus used this phrase when He was speaking to Peter and Andrew. He saw them when they were beginning to fish in a lake, and Jesus told them to follow Him. He said that He would make them "fishers of men." "Unlike the actual process of fishing where the fish is taken out of the sea of life, here humanity is saved from the sea of sins and renewed in body, mind, and spirit through the waters of Baptism. This is done by none other than the 'fishers of men' who are empowered by none other than Christ Jesus. As you have probably noticed, Jesus chose men who were not exactly fit to be spiritual leaders at the time. They were poor, uneducated, weak, self-centered, and clearly lacked the qualities that a true teacher should possess. However, Jesus told them, 'Follow me, and **I will make you** fishers of men.' He did not choose them based on what they already were, but what He could make out of them if they decided to follow His footsteps. This is the love of the Lord, for when you decide to follow His will, He blesses you with a gift of transformation, such that it is not only you who sees the light, but you become the light for others to guide them through darkness" (Reference: https://spiritualray.com/what-is-meaning-of-fishers-of-men-phrase/ What is the Meaning of 'Fishers of Men' Phrase? Elaborated Here/ Shalu Bhatti).

- "ASK AND IT WILL BE GIVEN" (MATTHEW 7:7, LUKE 11:9): A lot of people look at this scripture and just assume that it means you can literally ask God for anything, like He's a genie and He'll just give it to—FALSE! If you do a little bit of digging and research, the passages mean you can ask for anything that ALIGNS WITH GOD'S WILL FOR YOUR LIFE. He won't give you anything that will hurt you, that you'll put before Him, or that goes against His will. "You may ask me for anything in my name, and I will do it." Here, Jesus does not promise His disciples anything and everything they want; rather, He instructs them to ask 'in my name.' To pray in Jesus' name is to pray on the basis of Jesus' authority, but it also involves praying according to the will of God, for the will of God is what Jesus always did (John 6:38). This truth is stated explicitly in 1 John 5:14, 'If we ask anything according to his will, he hears us." Our requests must be congruent with the will of God'" (Reference: https://www.gotquestions.org/ask-and-you-shall-receive.html/ What Did Jesus Mean When He said, "Ask and you shall receive?).

- "HE WILL GIVE YOU THE DESIRES OF YOUR HEART" (PSALM 37:4): This kind of goes along with the last scripture I went over. "If we truly find satisfaction and worth in Christ, Scripture says He will give us the longings of our hearts. Does that mean, if we go to church every Sunday, God will give us a new Rolls Royce? No. The idea behind this verse and others like it is that, when we truly rejoice or 'delight' in the eternal things of God, our desires will begin to parallel His and we will never go unfulfilled. Matthew 6:33 says, 'But seek first his kingdom and his righteousness, and all these things [the necessities of life] will be given to you as well.'" (Reference: https://www.gotquestions.org/delight-yourself-in-the-Lord.html/ What Does It Mean to Delight Yourself in the Lord?/ Psalm 37:4). In short, when you put God first, He will begin to align you with His will and place new desires in your heart.

- "JUDGE NOT LEST YE BE NOT JUDGED" (MATTHEW 7:1-3): "He didn't mean we should never make a judgment about right and wrong. As He explained, He meant we shouldn't make a judgment hypocritically. The verses that follow make this patently clear (Matthew 7:3-5). We know no one is perfect, but we expect it anyway. Except in ourselves. We often excuse our own shortcomings because we claim God's grace. But then we turn around and demand others be perfect—a standard we ourselves don't meet. This is precisely what Jesus was warning against" (Reference: https://waynestiles.com/judge-not-lest-ye-be-judged-what-jesus-meant/ Judge Not, Lest Ye Be Judged—What Jesus Meant/ Wayne Stiles).

COMMON SYMBOLISM
- SHEEP/SHEPHERD—This symbolism is deep. It blew my mind when I learned about all this. In the Bible, there are countless scriptures illustrating God and the Lord Jesus being our Shepherd and man (us) as His sheep. What's the significance of it? Look at the roles and behavior of both sheep and shepherds.
    - SHEEP:
        - "Sheep are not bright animals, or defensive ones. They need lots of care". (Reference: http://www.djournal.com/lifestyle/the-metaphor-of-the-shepherd-holds-deep-

implications-for-christ/article_9015c04b-dc9a-57c2-9ed4-d193857453e4.html/ The Metaphor of the Shepherd Holds Deep Implications for Christ/ Pastors/ Riley Manning).

- "I have often heard that sheep are among the simplest of livestock. That is to say, sheep are quite vulnerable without a shepherd. They are vulnerable to their enemies, such as wolves and the thieves mentioned in John 10. They are also vulnerable to themselves as they tend to wander from the flock" (Reference: https://www.ministrymatters.com/all/entry/2622/sheep-need-a-shepherd/ Sheep Need a Shepherd/ Tracey Allred).

- SHEPHERD:
  - "The Rev. Keith Cochran, pastor of West Jackson Street Baptist Church, said shepherds ranked pretty low on the cultural hierarchy. They were seen as rough, dirty, spending days, even weeks, out under the stars with their animals. For Cochran, there's as much to be learned from the sheep themselves as their caretakers" (Reference: http://www.djournal.com/lifestyle/the-metaphor-of-the-shepherd-holds-deep-

implications-for-christ/article_9015c04b-dc9a-57c2-9ed4-d193857453e4.html/ The Metaphor of the Shepherd Holds Deep Implications for Christ, Pastors", Riley Manning).

- A shepherd would put their flocks' lives over his own. He protects them with his rod against other animals or thieves.
- "…the good shepherd showed great concern for his sheep. He provided for them in terms of nourishment and rest. He guided them, leading the way. He was intimately involved with the flock and concerned for the safety of each individual. He was willing to sacrifice his own comfort, even his own life, for the sake of his sheep" (Reference: https://www.xenos.org/essays/shepherd-motif-old-and-new-testament/ The Shepherd Motif in the Old and New Testament/ Mary Beth Gladwell).

Do you see a connection yet? Let's break it down.

1. If we are the sheep and sheep are said to wander away from the flock and from their shepherd easily, it could symbolize a couple of things. It could refer to us wandering away from God's will for our lives and He has to come bring us back on the right track. It could mean mankind wandering away from God's perfect

design of life and living to please our flesh, while God is trying to call us back to Him.

2. If sheep are said not to be the brightest animals, what does that mean about us? Not to say that we are stupid, but as humans, we do make mistakes—a lot of times we repeat the same mistakes. We can be lured away from God's will if the enemy presents something to us the right way; we can fall back into our old destructive habits after receiving salvation. "...sheep are notorious for following the leader, regardless of how dangerous or foolish that may be. Like sheep, human beings are extremely gullible when an attractive or charismatic leader promises a shiny new idea. History is replete with tragic illustrations of the 'herd mentality' in action (Acts 13:50; 19:34; Numbers 16:2). That sheep-like mentality was in evidence when Pilate brought Jesus before the people to ask what should be done with Him. Only days before, Jesus had been the popular Teacher who healed, forgave, and taught about God. People eagerly followed Him. But, less than a week later, 'the chief priests stirred up the crowd to have Pilate release Barabbas instead' (Mark 15:11). Within moments, the very crowd that had witnessed His miracles was shouting, 'Crucify Him!'" (Reference: https://www.gotquestions.org/sheep-in-the-Bible.html). And at the same time, we like to act like we have it all together and we know what is best for our lives. We need a GOOD shepherd. Compared to

an all-knowing God who created us and knew each one of us before birth, we don't know anything. We need that guidance to navigate this life.

3. If sheep are vulnerable to wolves, how does that relate to us? If Satan is the ruler of this world, that means we are on his territory. There is a chance of an attack every single day. I don't know about you, but I want to make sure that I am protected. We need a shepherd to be those watchful eyes for us if the enemy wants to try and come for us.

Okay now, what about the shepherd?

1. Shepherds are said to have a very dangerous job. They had to make sure that their sheep were protected against thieves and even wild animals (this is why they used a staff to protect them). It meant putting their lives on the line for the sake of their flock—remember what Jesus did for you and me?

2. The shepherd's job was dirty as well because they had to make sure that their sheep's wool stayed clean. It's a job that not a lot of people want to do. When Jesus was in the middle of His ministry, He associated with the sick, blind people who, by society's standards at the time, were not supposed to be socialized with. And if you want to take it a step further, He, a perfect being with no blemish on Him, came to US, a dirty, sin-filled people, and He did this in order to save us from

ourselves.

3. Shepherds took the time out to know each one of the sheep that were in their flock. He knew which ones had the tendency to wander off at certain times and which ones spooked easily at night. The Lord knows every single one of us intimately and by name! He knows our strengths, weaknesses and what makes us tick. He did create us, after all.

I seriously recommend that you read Psalm 23. Make sure to read it slowly, dissecting every single line. Every single verse in this psalm clearly demonstrates how God is our Great Shepherd. I swear it is so crazy how much you miss when you just rush through this.

I know that it kind of sucks hearing that we, as humans, are compared to one of the dumbest animals on the Earth. Especially now with more people trying to be "woke" and enlightened, everyone is saying "Don't be a sheep" and follow everyone else. Meaning don't just fall for anything you hear; don't follow the crowd just because everyone else is doing it. But hey, if we're really honest with ourselves, like sheep, we naturally wander and rebel. We're stubborn and need leadership. We are not all-knowing beings; we cannot even fully comprehend the purpose of life itself. So, how in the world can we go through this life without a shepherd? We're all sheep following a shepherd of some sort. We just follow different ones. Are you following the one who is leading you to eternal life or the one that leads to death? Let's stop pretending that we're these beings that have all of this knowledge of the universe hidden in us. Compared to the all-knowing, all-powerful Creator of the universe, we know absolutely nothing. Time to humble ourselves and accept that we are sheep, and we need the Great Shepherd to lead us. What shepherd are you following?

- VALLEY/WILDERNESS/MOUNTAINTOP—Valleys and the wildernesses represent struggle, difficulties, tests, and trials. Mountaintops represent victory and blessings.

- CIRCUMSISED—In the Old Testament, circumcision was required of the Israelites (Abraham's descendants) to represent the covenant between them and God. Circumcision of the heart, on the other hand, means a peeling away of the flesh and becoming pure of heart. "Paul is discussing the role of the Old Testament Law as it relates to Christianity. He argues that Jewish circumcision is only an outward sign of being set apart to God. However, if the heart is sinful, then physical circumcision is of no avail. A circumcised body and a sinful heart are at odds with each other. Rather than focus on external rites, Paul focuses on the condition of the heart. Using circumcision as a metaphor, he says that only the Holy Spirit can purify a heart and set us apart to God. Ultimately, circumcision cannot make a person right with God; the Law is not enough. A person's heart must change. Paul calls this change "circumcision of the heart" (Reference: https://www.gotquestions.org/circumcision-of-the-heart.html/ What is Circumcision of the Heart?)_. This ties back into how the Old Testament is filled with laws to stay close to God and the New Testament ties to Jesus' coming so we don't have to follow rules to have a relationship with Him. Just accept Christ as your Savior from sin.

- CLAY/POTTER—"Although God allows human beings freedom to make moral choices, He demonstrates often that He is still sovereign and in control of His universe. He does whatever He wills with His creation (Psalm 135:6; 155:3; Daniel 4:35; Isaiah 46:9–11). We need frequent reminders that God is over all and can do as He pleases whether we understand His actions or not (Romans 9:20–21). He owes us nothing yet chooses to extend to us the utmost patience, kindness, and compassion (Jeremiah 9:24; Psalm 36:10; 103:4, 17). The potter working with the clay reminds us that God is at work in us "for His good pleasure" (Philippians 2:13). Isaiah 45:9 says, "Woe to those who quarrel with their Maker, those who are nothing but potsherds among the potsherds on the ground. Does the clay say to the potter, 'What are you making?' Does your work say, 'The potter has no hands'?"

God has created each of us the way He wants us (Psalm 139:13–16; Exodus 4:11). It is our responsibility to take what He has given us and use it for His glory and pleasure. In doing so, we find our ultimate fulfillment. Rather than live with disappointment and dissatisfaction with what

God has or has not given us, we can choose to thank Him in everything (Ephesians 5:20; Colossians 3:15). Just as the clay finds its highest purpose when it remains pliable in the hands of the potter, so our lives fulfill their highest purpose when we let our Potter have His way with us " (Reference: https://www.gotquestions.org/potter-and-clay.html).

- DOVE/HOLY SPIRIT
    - "Because the Holy Spirit is just that—spirit—He is not visible to us. On this occasion, however, the Spirit took on a visible appearance and was undoubtedly seen by the people. The dove is an emblem of purity and harmlessness (Matthew 10:16), and the form of the dove at Jesus' baptism signified that the Spirit with which Jesus was endowed was one of holiness and innocence.
    - Another symbol involving the dove comes from the account of the Flood and Noah's ark in Genesis 6-8. When the earth had been covered with water for some time, Noah wanted to check to see if there was dry land anywhere, so he sent out a dove from the ark; the dove came back with an olive branch in her beak (Genesis 8:11). Since that time, the olive branch has been a symbol of peace. Symbolically, the story of Noah's dove tells us that God declared peace with mankind after the Flood had purged the earth of its wickedness. The dove represented His Spirit bringing the good news of the reconciliation

of God and man. Of course, this was only a temporal reconciliation, because lasting, spiritual reconciliation with God only comes through Jesus Christ. But it is significant that the Holy Spirit was pictured as a dove at Jesus' baptism, thereby once again symbolizing peace with God" (Reference: https://www.gotquestions.org/Holy-Spirit-dove.html/ Why is The Dove Often Used As a Symbol For the Holy Spirit?).

LIST OF GOD'S AND JESUS' NAMES
GOD

- "I AM THAT I AM"— "When God identified Himself as I AM WHO I AM, He stated that, no matter when or where, He is there. It is similar to the New Testament expression in Revelation 1:8, "'I am the Alpha and the Omega,' says the Lord God, 'who is, and who was, and who is to come, the Almighty.'" This is true of Him for all time, but it would have been especially appropriate for a message in Moses' day to a people in slavery and who could see no way out. I AM was promising to free them, and they could count on Him!" (Reference: https://www.gotquestions.org/I-AM-WHO-I-AM-Exodus-3-14.html,/ What is The Meaning of I AM WHO I AM in Exodus 3:14?).

- "THE GREAT I AM"—He is saying that He is infinite. He has always been and always will be. He has no beginning and no end. "God's name is in the present tense; He says, 'I am,' not 'I was x, but am now y.' Our values or knowledge change, but the Lord remains the same (James 1:17). He is never inconsistent; we can therefore count on His wrath for sinners and His mercy for the repentant" (Reference: https://www.ligonier.org/learn/devotionals/great-i-am/ The Great I AM).

- "LORD"—"...when 'LORD' in all caps or small caps occurs in the Old Testament, it is a replacement for an occurrence of God's Hebrew name 'YHWH,' also known as the *Tetragrammaton*. This is fairly consistent throughout all the different English translations of the Bible. When 'Lord' occurs in the Old Testament, referring to God, it is usually a rendering of 'Adonai,' a name/title of God that emphasizes His lordship. LORD/YHWH and Lord/Adonai are by far the two most consistent renderings throughout all the different English Bible translations" (Reference: https://www.gotquestions.org/LORD-GOD-Lord-God.html/ What Do LORD, GOD, Lord, God, etc., Stand for in the Bible?).

- "LORD"—(Deuteronomy 6:4; Daniel 9:14) – strictly speaking, the only proper name for God. Translated in English Bibles 'LORD' (all capitals) to distinguish it from *Adonai*, 'Lord.' The revelation of the name is given to Moses 'I Am who I Am' (Exodus 3:14). This name specifies an immediacy, a presence. Yahweh is present, accessible, near to those who call on Him for deliverance (Psalm 107:13), forgiveness (Psalm 25:11) and guidance (Psalm 31:3)"

- (Reference: https://www.gotquestions.org/names-of-God.html/ What Are The Different Names of God, and What Do They Mean?)

- "JEHOVAH"— "The vast majority of Jewish and Christian biblical scholars and linguists do not believe "Jehovah" to be the proper pronunciation of *YHWH*. There was no true *J* sound in ancient Hebrew. Even the Hebrew letter *vav*, which is transliterated as the *W* in *YHWH* is said to have originally had a pronunciation closer to *W* than the *V* of *Jehovah*. *Jehovah* is essentially a Germanic pronunciation of the Latinized transliteration of the Hebrew *YHWH*. It is the letters of the tetragrammaton, Latinized into *JHVH*, with vowels inserted (Reference: https://www.gotquestions.org/Jehovah.html/ Is Jehovah The True Name of God?).

- "ADONAI"—"Lord" (Genesis 15:2; Judges 6:15) – used in place of YHWH, which was thought by the Jews to be too sacred to be uttered by sinful men. In the Old Testament, YHWH is more often used in God's dealings with His people, while *Adonai* is used more when He deals with the Gentiles" (Reference: https://www.gotquestions.org/names-of-God.html/ What Are The Different Names of God, and What Do They Mean?).

- "EL"—"EL" is another name used for God in the Bible, showing up about 200 times in the Old Testament. *El* is the simple form arising from *Elohim*, and is often combined with other words for descriptive emphasis (Reference: https://www.allaboutgod.com/names-of-god.htm/ Names of God).

- "EL ELYON [el-el-*yohn*]"—'Most High' (Deuteronomy 26:19) – derived from the Hebrew root for 'go up' or 'ascend,' so the implication is of that which is the very highest. *El Elyon* denotes exaltation and speaks of absolute right to lordship" (Reference: https://www.gotquestions.org/names-of-God.html/ What Are The Different Names of God, and What Do They Mean?).

- "EL ROI [el-roh-*ee*]"—'God of Seeing' (Genesis 16:13) – the name ascribed to God by Hagar, alone and desperate in the wilderness after being driven out by Sarah (Genesis 16:1-14). When Hagar met the Angel of the Lord, she realized she had seen God Himself in a theophany. She also realized that *El Roi* saw her in her distress and testified that He is a God who lives and sees all" (Reference: https://www.gotquestions.org/names-of-God.html/ What Are The Different Names of God, and What Do They Mean?).

- "EL-OLAM [el-oh-*lahm*]"—'Everlasting God' (Psalm 90:1-3) – God's nature is without beginning or end, free from all constraints of time, and He contains within Himself the very cause of time itself. 'From everlasting to everlasting, You are God' (Reference:

https://www.gotquestions.org/names-of-God.html/ What Are The Different Names of God, and What Do They Mean?).

- "EL-GIBHOR [el-ghee-*bohr*]"—"Mighty God" (Isaiah 9:6) – the name describing the Messiah, Christ Jesus, in this prophetic portion of Isaiah. As a powerful and mighty warrior, the Messiah, the Mighty God, will accomplish the destruction of God's enemies and rule with a rod of iron (Revelation 19:15)" (Reference: https://www.gotquestions.org/names-of-God.html/ What Are The Different Names of God, and What Do They Mean?).

- "ELOHIM"— God 'Creator, Mighty and Strong' (Genesis 17:7; Jeremiah 31:33) – the plural form of *Eloah*, which accommodates the doctrine of the Trinity. From the Bible's first sentence, the superlative nature of God's power is evident as God (Elohim) speaks the world into existence (Genesis 1:1)" (Reference: https://www.gotquestions.org/names-of-God.html/ What Are The Different Names of God, and What Do They Mean?).

- "JEHOVAH JIREH"—The Lord will provide

- "JEHOVAH NISSI"—The Lord is my banner "A banner is something that identifies and unifies a particular group of people. For example, a military flag or standard is sometimes called a banner. The Israelites' saying, 'The Lord is my Banner,' was a way of identifying themselves as the unified followers of the Lord God. A banner also functions as a rallying point for troops in a battle." (Reference: https://www.gotquestions.org/Lord-is-my-banner.html/ What Does it Mean That the Lord is my Banner?).

- "JEHOVAH/YAHWEH RAPHA"—The Lord who heals

- "JEHOVAH/YAHWEH M'KADDESH"—The Lord who sanctifies, makes holy

- "JEHOVAH/YAHWEH SHALOM"—The Lord our peace

- "JEHOVAH/YAHWEH SABAOTH"—"The Lord of Hosts" (Isaiah 1:24; Psalm 46:7) – *Hosts* means 'hordes,' both of angels and of men. He is Lord of the host of heaven and of the inhabitants of the earth, of Jews and Gentiles, of rich and poor, master and slave. The name is expressive of the majesty, power, and authority of God and shows that He is able to accomplish what He determines to do" (Reference: http://www.fbcgahanna.org/names-of-god/ Names of God).

- "JEHOVAH/YAHWEH SHAMMAH"—The Lord is there

- "JEHOVAH/YAHWEH ROHI"—The Lord, our Shepherd

- "JEHOVAH/YAHWEH TSIDKENU"—The Lord, our Righteousness

- "JEHOVAH/YAHWEH ELOHIM"—LORD God

JESUS

- "THE SEVEN "I AM'S"—These "I Am's" remind us that Jesus is an infinite being just like God, the Father. God tells Moses when he is at the burning bush to call Him "I Am that I Am" and Jesus is using the same phrase! Deep, right? "In all seven, He combines I AM with tremendous metaphors which express His saving relationship toward the world. All appear in the book of John. They are I AM the Bread of Life (John 6:35, 41, 48, 51); I AM the Light of the World (John 8:12); I AM the Door of the Sheep (John 10:7, 9); I AM the Good Shepherd (John 10:11,14); I AM the Resurrection and the Life (John 11:25); I AM the Way, the Truth and the Life (John 14:6); and I AM the True Vine (John 15:1, 5) " (Reference: https://www.gotquestions.org/I-AM.html/ What Did Jesus Mean When He said 'I AM'?).

- "BRIDEGROOM"—A bridegroom is a man who has just married or is about to be married. "A bridegroom is the male version of a bride, a woman who is just married or just about to be married. The word *bridegroom* comes from the Old English *brydguma*, which was a combination of *bryd* ("bride") and *guma* ("man"). The word *bridegroom* appears in the Bible in both Testaments and carries the same meaning: the husband of the bride.'"' ... John the Baptist presented himself as the 'friend who attends the bridegroom,' which is the person we would today call the 'best man' (John 3:29). John said, 'The bride belongs to the bridegroom,' and by this he referred to Jesus and the church, His spiritual bride, who stands by His side and invites people in, saying, "'Come!' Let the one who is thirsty come; and let the one who wishes take the free gift of the water of life" (Revelation 22:17). This church—the Bride of Christ—is not one specific local church or denomination but the entire body of believers throughout the ages. All who have trusted the Lord and received salvation by grace through faith are collectively His Bride. This analogy exists in several New Testament passages. Paul gives believers instructions about marriage, saying, 'Husbands, love your wives, just as Christ loved the church and gave himself up for her' (Ephesians 5:25). Paul also refers to the church as a virgin waiting for her bridegroom (2 Corinthians 11:2) and uses the relationship between Christ and the church as an example of the importance of wives' submission to their husbands (Ephesians 5:24)" (Reference: https://www.gotquestions.org/bridegroom.html/ What is a Bridegroom?).

- "THE VINE"—"Jesus goes on to explain that He is a vine whose branches must bear fruit or they will be cut off by the Father (John 15:2). The branches that do bear fruit will be pruned to increase their yield (15:2). The branches of the true vine, like the branches of a grape vine, must be pruned so that the harvest will be more abundant. Jesus is the vine and we are the branches (15:5). Through hardship, discipline, and suffering, we are pruned so that our fruit will be ever greater and ever sweeter. The Father prunes us if we abide in Christ. Those that do not abide are the branches that are cut off (15:6). If we abide in Christ and bear fruit we can know that we are truly His. Some are cut off because they are not His — they try to attach themselves to Christ without abiding in Him through faith. But those who bear fruit are His, and they have been cleansed by Him (15:3). They will not be cut off. Those who bear no fruit are just dead wood and were never truly a part of the vine to begin with." (Reference: https://www.ligonier.org/learn/devotionals/true-vine/ The True Vine).

- "JACOB'S LADDER"—In Genesis, while Jacob is traveling from one city to another, he lays down to rest somewhere and has a dream. In it, he sees a ladder reaching from Heaven to Earth and angels were going up and down on it. Guess who represents the ladder? Jesus is our way of connecting to God and Heaven, so Jacob's God-given dream was a foreshadowing of Jesus paving the way for us to God!
- "LAMB OF GOD"—In the Old Testament, the Israelites were required to give a sacrifice in place of their sins in order to maintain a relationship with God. Like I've explained in the book, Jesus acted as our sacrifice when He

was nailed to the cross and took on our past, present, and future sins. This name is a reminder to us of how God provided a sacrifice for us in the form of His only Son.

- LILY OF THE VALLEY
    - "A lily is a sweet and a fragrant flower, yet of such a strong and odoriferous scent that a man's senses (naturalists say) will be easily overturned with the sweet savour thereof. The Lord Jesus Christ may vary fitly be compared to the lily, whose savour and spiritual sweetness very much excels and transcends the sweetest of any odours that can be mentioned; and honey and the honey-comb are sweet to the smell, and sweeter to the taste: O then how sweet is the precious savour of our blessed Saviour!
    - A lily is white and very beautiful; within it are seven grains or seeds, of the color of gold, so amiable that our Saviour saith, "That even Solomon in all his glory was not arrayed like one of these." For whiteness it exceeds all flowers. Whiteness denotes holiness; it is said of the bride, the Lamb's wife, "And to her was granted that she should be arrayed in fine linen, clean and white: for the fine linen is the righteousness of saints." *Revelation 19:8*. And of those "Thou hast a few names even in Sardis which have not defiled their garments; and they shall walk with me in white: for they are worthy." *Revelation 3:4* Purity is essential,

originally, perfectly, and absolutely inherent in Christ; He is holiness itself, His glory is infinite, within and without, every way glorious; the perfection of beauty.

- It is observed that the lily is exceeding fruitful; one root puts forth fifty bulbs or scallions. Jesus Christ is exceeding fruitful, from this Root, (for so is He called) how many lilies, or holy, and heavenly churches, have there sprung? Yea, from this blessed lily many thousands of holy and sanctified Christians.
- The lily is the tallest of flowers yet hangs down its head. Jesus Christ is higher than the mighty princes, kings and emperors of the earth, higher than heaven or angels, and yet humble and lowly in heart; therefore He is compared to the lily of the valley, in His exaltations, as God very high; but in His humiliations, He seems to hang down His head.
- The lily is a flower that hath many medicinal virtues; the distilled water of a lily is good to restore a lost voice, it helps faintness, is good for the liver, helps the dropsy; and the oil of it is good for divers maladies, says Galen. The great and incomparable virtue that is in the Lord Jesus Christ, is excellently good to cure all the diseases and maladies of the soul; it cures spiritual blindness, it softens a hard heart, it cures stubbornness and obstinacy, by His blessed infusion of grace; in a word, there is no malady too hard for this spiritual

Physician" (Reference: http://www.learnthebible.org/christ-the-lily-of-the-valley.html/ Christ the Lily of the Valley/ Benjamin Keech).

- "YESHUA" — "The answer lies in the fact that the origins of 'Yeshua' and where it is used most to describe Jesus draws believers closer to the realization of what He came to do on earth and in heaven. It's a name that represents His Hebrew identity and establishes a stronger connection with believers of all generations."... "First, it is the understanding that 'Yeshua' is a more personal name of Jesus because it originated in the lifetime that Jesus was alive on Earth. The use of 'Yeshua' in Hebrew text connects more to when Jesus emerged in the presence of those around Him, as well as Hebrew being mentioned, earlier, as the holy language. Those who were fluent in Hebrew, Greek, and Aramaic would decipher that 'Yeshua' meant 'deliverer, savior,' and realize this man was more than just a man. Coupled with His behavior and spiritual connection with God, those around Him would see that He was different from others and this probably led to Him being loved by some and hated by others" (Reference: https://www.biblestudytools.com/bible-study/topical-studies/yeshua-deliverer-savior.html/ Yeshua: Deliverer, Savior - Why This Name of God is So Important for Today/ Blair Parke).

- "KING OF KINGS AND LORD OF LORDS"—"In Revelation 19:16 Jesus is given the full title "KING OF KINGS AND LORD OF LORDS" (Revelation 17:14 switches it: "Lord of lords and King of kings"). The title indicates someone who has the power to exercise absolute dominion over all His realm. In the case of the Lord Jesus, the realm is all of creation. In John's vision, Jesus is returning to judge the world and establish His earthly kingdom, as He predicted in Mark 13:26. When Jesus is called 'King of kings and Lord of lords,' it means that, in the end, all other rulers will be conquered or abolished, and He alone will reign supreme as King and Lord of all the earth. There is no power, no king, and no lord who can oppose Him and win" (Reference: https://www.gotquestions.org/King-of-kings-Lord-of-lords.html/ What Does It Mean That Jesus is King of Kings and Lord of Lords?).

- "THE DOOR"—Let's go back to how Jesus is the Good Shepherd. When a shepherd is watching over his flock, oftentimes, the sheep are placed in a pen or a sheepfold. On this pen, there is only one door for the shepherd to come in and go out. Jesus serves as our door to the sheepfold because He makes sure that we are protected from any outside threats, and once we are in, He will not let us out of His sight! He is also saying that He is the only way to full protection from the enemy and death! "In this context, Jesus is telling us that He is not only the shepherd of the sheep, but also the door of the sheep. In doing so, He is vividly contrasting Himself with that of the religious leaders of His time whom He describes as 'thieves and robbers' (John 10:8). When Jesus says, 'I am the door,' He is reiterating the fact that only through Him is salvation possible. This is far removed from the ecumenical teachings popular in today's liberal religious circles. Jesus makes it clear that any religious leader who offers salvation other than the teachings of Christ is a 'thief' and a 'robber'" (Reference: https://www.gotquestions.org/I-am-the-door.html/ What Did Jesus Mean When He Said "I am the door" (John 10:7)?).

- "CHIEF CORNERSTONE"—In ancient times, the cornerstone of a building was the part that held everything together. It was placed in the right corner of the building and served as the foundation. "Jesus describes Himself as the Cornerstone that His church would be built upon, a unified body of believers, both Jew and Gentile. The Book of Isaiah has many references to the Messiah to come. In several places He is referred to as 'the Cornerstone,' such as in Isaiah 28:16-17: "So this is what the sovereign Lord says: 'See, I lay a stone in Zion, a tested stone, a precious cornerstone for a sure foundation; the one who trusts will never be dismayed. I will make justice the measuring line and righteousness the plumb line.'" God is speaking to scoffers and boasters when He refers to the Cornerstone—His precious Son—who provides the firm foundation for their lives, if they would but trust in Him" (Reference: https://www.gotquestions.org/Jesus-Christ-cornerstone.html/ What Does It Mean That Jesus Christ is the Cornerstone?).

- "LION OF JUDAH"—"Based on Jacob's blessing, the lion is a symbol of the tribe of Judah, which is known as the kingly tribe (King David was of the tribe of Judah). Lions symbolize power, fierceness, and majesty. Lions are the king of the beasts, and the Lion of the tribe of Judah is the king of everything. In the Old Testament, God is sometimes described as being like a lion. In Isaiah 31:4, just 'as a lion growls, a great lion over its prey—and though a whole band of shepherds is called together against it, it is not frightened by their shouts . . . so the LORD Almighty will come down to do battle on Mount Zion and on its heights.' The Lord is not afraid of His enemies. He protects His people and does not allow them to be conquered. In Hosea, God is angry at Israel because they became proud and forgot Him. God says, 'I will be like a lion to them. . . .. like a lion I will devour them. . . .. You are destroyed, Israel, because you are against me, against your helper' (Hosea 13:7–8). It is better to experience the help and protection of the Lion than to deny His kingship and face His fierceness. In Revelation 5, Jesus is the long-awaited Lion of the tribe of Judah. John weeps because no one was found worthy to open the scroll of God's judgment or even to look inside it. Then one of the elders says to John, 'Do not weep! See, the Lion of the tribe of Judah, the Root of David, has triumphed. He is able to open the scroll and its seven seals' (Revelation 5:4–5).

Both of the genealogies in Matthew and Luke record that Jesus is a descendant of the tribe of Judah. When Jesus is revealed as the promised Lion of the tribe of Judah, it reveals His deity. He is the true king and the One to whom belongs the long-awaited obedience of nations. Yet it is not His fierceness or the force of His power that makes Him worthy. The Lion has triumphed because He became a Lamb (Revelation 5:6–10; cf. John 1:29). Jesus Christ is worthy because He lived a perfect, sinless life and in shedding His blood defeated sin and death. His death and resurrection have resulted in a protection for His people and an eternal kingdom that will honor and worship God. Ruling this kingdom will be Jesus, the Lion of the tribe of Judah" (Reference: https://www.gotquestions.org/lion-tribe-Judah.html/ Who/What is the Lion of the Tribe of Judah?).

THE HOLY SPIRIT

- "PARACLETE" -- "This word occurs 5 times in the New Testament, all in the writings of John. Four instances are in the Gospel and one in the First Epistle. In the Gospel the in the Epistle, 1 John 2:1. 'Paraclete' is simply the Greek word transferred into English. The translation of the word in English Versions of the Bible is 'Comforter' in the Gospel, and 'Advocate' in the Epistle. The Greek word is parakletos, froth the verb parakaleo. The word for "Paraclete" is passive in form, and etymologically signifies "called to one's side."

    In general, the word signifies:

(1) a legal advocate, or counsel for defense,
(2) an intercessor,
(3) a helper, generally "(Reference: https://www.biblestudytools.com/dictionary/paraclete/ Paraclete).

MY LAST PRAYER FOR YOU

Heavenly Father, you know where every person reading this book is in his or her life right now. You have blessed every one of them with the chance to be able to make it to this point in their lives. Father, in the name of your Holy Son, Jesus Christ, I ask that you please speak to their hearts and minds and reveal Your plan for their lives. Let them know that it is never too late to accept Christ as their Savior. Let Your love seep deep into their lives, penetrating every deep wound that they have. Allow them to experience the beauty of Your holiness and the peace of Your presence. Give them a glimpse into what their lives can be like if they put You first. Reveal and dismantle any plans the enemy has for their lives. Lord, reverse the curse in the name of Jesus! I pray that from this day forward, each person reading this book will encounter only people who will push them to pursue a deeper relationship with You and who will enhance their view of the church. I pray this prayer with the belief that it will come to pass! IN JESUS NAME, I PRAY! AND LET IT BE SO—AMEN! Much love!

My Unanswered Questions

www.ingramcontent.com/pod-product-compliance
Lightning Source LLC
LaVergne TN
LVHW051544070426
835507LV00021B/2389